The Renewal of the Kibbutz

The Renewal of the Kibbutz

From Reform to Transformation

RAYMOND RUSSELL,
ROBERT HANNEMAN,
AND SHLOMO GETZ

RUTGERS UNIVERSITY PRESS

NEW BRUNSWICK, NEW JERSEY, AND LONDON

LIBRARY OF CONGRESS CATALOGING-IN-PUBLICATION DATA

Russell, Raymond.

The renewal of the kibbutz : from reform to transformation / Raymond Russell, Robert Hanneman, Shlomo Getz.

p. cm.

Includes bibliographical references and index.

ISBN 978–0–8135–6076–2 (hardcover : alk. paper) — ISBN 978–0–8135–6077–9 (e-book)/

1. Kibbutzim. I. Hanneman, Robert. II. Getz, Shlomo. III. Title.

HX742.2.A3R87 2013

307.77'6—dc23   2012033356

A British Cataloging-in-Publication record for this book is available from the British Library.

Visit our website: http://rutgerspress.rutgers.edu

Manufactured in the United States of America

To Menachem Rosner, for contributing so much to kibbutz
research, and for inviting us to join him in the study of the kibbutz

CONTENTS

TABLES

ACKNOWLEDGMENTS

This volume is the result of more than two decades of research. In the course of assembling the information presented here, we have accumulated debts to a large number of people.

Our greatest debt is to Menachem Rosner. As a researcher, Rosner has been extraordinarily original and productive. He was one of the earliest scholars to write about many of the issues and changes addressed in this work. When Getz and Russell first showed interest in kibbutz research, Rosner served as a mentor to them both, tutoring each as needed on literatures and controversies affecting the kibbutzim. Later, it was Rosner who introduced Getz and Russell to each other, in 1995, and suggested that they explore the possibility of working together.

We also have many debts to other current and former colleagues at the Institute for Research of the Kibbutz at the University of Haifa. Michal Palgi has provided help and encouragement at every stage of this project. We are especially grateful to Michal Palgi and to Shaul Sharir and Elliette Orchan for access to the results of their annual polls of kibbutz members. Other colleagues at the Institute who have provided helpful advice or information during the years of this study include Gila Adar, Chanah Goldenberg, Uri Leviatan, Avraham Pavin, and Dani Rosolio.

We would also like to thank a number of other specialists studying or advising kibbutzim or other communes, who shared with us their knowledge and insights about these institutions. These expert informants include Shulamit Arbel, Eli Avrahami, Eliezer Ben-Rafael, Gary Brenner, Shlomo Cohen, Yechezkel Dar, James Grant-Rosenhead, Tal Israeli, Baruch Kanari, Michael Livni, Anton Marks, Henry Near, Yaacov Oved, Israel Oz,

Alon Pauker, Menachem Topel, Israel Tsufim, Muki Tsur, Tal Simons, and Eppie Yaar.

Hundreds of kibbutz general secretaries or other office holders responded to the Institute's annual surveys of changes on kibbutzim from 1990 to 2001. Many other kibbutz members provided interviews or made presentations about changes taking place on their own kibbutz. We would like to thank all of these kibbutz members for being so generous with their time and information. This research could not have been completed without their cooperation.

Ever since we first contacted Marlie Wasserman of Rutgers University Press about this manuscript, she has treated it with the highest professionalism and efficiency. We are also grateful to Margo Crouppen and several anonymous reviewers for helpful comments on earlier drafts.

Finally, we would like to thank our wives, Judy Lehr, Patricia Hanneman, and Eva Getz. A project of this size cannot be completed without causing numerous absences and distractions in the lives of everyone in the households involved. When the project stretches over multiple decades, the families affected are called upon to show extraordinary levels of forbearance. We are grateful to our wives for their patience and cooperation. We also owe special thanks to Judy Lehr for help with tables, editing, and the index.

The Renewal of the Kibbutz

INTRODUCTION

Perspectives on Change in the Kibbutzim

Since soon after their first appearance in Jewish Palestine in 1910, the collective rural settlements that later came to be known as "kibbutzim" have attracted international interest. At first, observers noted their unusually democratic and communal structures and practices. Although the land that each kibbutz was located on was the property of the Jewish National Fund, kibbutz members owned and operated other assets in common, working together in kibbutz-owned economic ventures, eating their meals in central dining halls, and living in kibbutz-owned housing. For Martin Buber (1958), common ownership of the means of both production and consumption made a kibbutz not only a producer cooperative and a consumer cooperative, but, more important, a "whole cooperative." In addition, all important decisions regarding both production and consumption were made by the General Assembly of the kibbutz, in which all members had an equal voice, and leadership positions were rotated. These practices have led others to see the kibbutzim as rare instances of direct democracy, or labor-managed firms. Finally, allocations from kibbutzim to their individual members followed the principle of "from each according to his or her ability, to each according to his or her need." This allowed kibbutz members to claim that they were not simply "building socialism," as were their counterparts in other countries; they were already practicing communism.

As years passed, the kibbutzim became known for another unique feature: they retained these unique structures and practices for long periods of time. Whereas most previous instances of communal and democratic

1

forms of work organization had either succumbed as businesses, or transformed themselves into conventional hierarchical organizations, the kibbutzim retained their structures and practices for many decades after they were formed. In Martin Buber's words, the kibbutzim stood out as "the experiment that did not fail."

Views of the kibbutzim both within and outside of Israel radically changed after 1985, when a sudden shift in government economic policy caught many kibbutzim with too much debt, leading to the collective bankruptcy of the entire kibbutz movement. As the kibbutzim negotiated with the government over new terms for their debt, pro-business politicians portrayed the kibbutz as a local instance of socialism, and recommended the same remedies for its ills that were growing in popularity throughout the world—namely, market-oriented reforms and privatization (Henisz, Zelner, and Guillen 2005). In the late 1980s, thousands of kibbutz members themselves began to share the widespread impression that the kibbutzim were no longer economically viable in their traditional form. Many left their kibbutzim entirely (Ben-Rafael 1997; Maron 1998; Mort and Brenner 2003). Others, like Yehuda Harel (1988), called for reforms that would lead to a "new kibbutz."

In the 1990s, the kibbutzim responded to these shocks and pressures by introducing a large number of reforms. Most kibbutzim transferred control of their economic ventures from the General Assembly to independent boards of directors. To manage those ventures, they began to employ outside experts, whom they paid substantial salaries. Most kibbutzim also either closed or reduced the hours of their common dining facilities, privatized costs of electricity, recreation, and many other forms of consumption, and began to allow kibbutz members to hold jobs outside the kibbutz.

In the last years of the 1990s and the early years of the new century, growing numbers of kibbutzim introduced a more radical change. Whereas all kibbutzim had previously lived by the principle of "from each according to his or her ability, to each according to his or her need," kibbutzim that adopted so-called safety-net budgets paid differential salaries to their members, based on the market value of each member's work. Sources both inside and outside the kibbutz movement viewed such changes as so substantial as to transform the kibbutzim that adopt them into entities barely recognizable as kibbutzim.

This book seeks to describe the changes that have occurred in the kibbutzim since 1990, and to identify the causes and significance of these changes. Thus the work pursues two complementary themes. On the one hand, it studies the extent to which the kibbutzim were in 1990, and remain, a unique set of organizations, sharing one or more characteristics that differentiate them from others; this perspective takes its inspiration from works that treat the kibbutz as a unique organizational form, or that see the kibbutzim as providing rare instances of an uncommon organizational form, such as direct democracy, cooperative production, or communal life. On the other hand, this book explores what kibbutzim have in common with other organizations, and asks whether kibbutzim have now become so similar to conventional organizations as to no longer be distinguishable from them. This latter perspective examines what general theories of organizations suggest are the most important circumstances under which organizations anywhere are most likely to introduce changes of any type. The analyses that follow demonstrate that, although both of these perspectives are relevant, it is the general theories of change in organizations that provide the better guide to the behavior of the kibbutzim in this period.

This chapter provides introductory information about each of these two perspectives.

Transformation of Alternative Organizations

To provide a complete account of how the kibbutzim are changing, this analysis begins by acknowledging ways the kibbutzim have historically been, and in many instances remain, unique. Recognizing the kibbutzim as unique entities begins with recognition of the special relationship between the kibbutzim and Israeli society. It is no accident that these organizations originated in this country; the kibbutzim were invented to meet the needs of Jewish immigrants to Palestine in the first half of the twentieth century. The challenge facing the kibbutzim today is to find ways to meet the needs of contemporary Israelis, while maintaining a shared and distinct identity.

Closely allied to the uniqueness of the kibbutzim is a set of general organizational traits or ideals for which the kibbutzim have been taken as rare examples. Kibbutzim have been described as uniquely democractic (Rosner and Cohen 1983), uniquely cooperative (Buber 1958), and uniquely communal organizations (Blasi 1978, 1986). It is these characteristics that have motivated large numbers of volunteers and tourists to visit the kibbutzim in the past (Mittelberg 1988). This work asks to what extent any or all of these labels still apply to the kibbutzim.

Whether we consider the kibbutzim of interest in themselves, or as examples of direct democracy, cooperatives, or communes, all of these terms refer to forms of organization that have been identified in prior studies as tending to transform themselves into organizations of more conventional types. In the literature on democracy, the classic statements are Robert Michels's (1962) "iron law of oligarchy" and Max Weber's (1978) analysis of the transformation of direct democracy into "rule by notables." Regarding cooperatives, Israeli perspectives (especially Preuss 1960) have been strongly influenced by the work of Franz Oppenheimer (1896), who saw cooperatives as subject to a "law of transformation." In the literature on communes, a similar perspective informs Donald Pitzer's (1989) theory of "developmental communalism."

In the literature on the kibbutzim, counterparts to these theories are provided by the work of such authors as Amitai Etzioni (1958), Eliezer Ben-Rafael (1988), Avner Ben-Ner (1987), and Erik Cohen (1983). In Cohen's essay "The Structural Transformation of the Kibbutzim" (1983) the author joined his teacher Yonina Talmon (1972) in seeing the communal kibbutz as illustrating Ferdinand Toennies's concept of *Gemeinschaft* ("community"). Writing in the 1970s, Cohen reported that, by that time, social relations in the kibbutzim had already begun to take on a different character, transforming the kibbutzim from instances of Gemeinschaft into instances of *Gesellschaft* ("association"). As kibbutz members came to differ from one another more in age, in work, in education, and in values, Cohen reported, they were becoming strangers to one another, and focusing increasingly on their own private households and careers.

In addition to sharing the idea that these forms of organizations are unusually short-lived, these literatures also share common thoughts about the influences that cause such groups to lose or abandon characteristics and practices that previously made them unique. In Weber's theory of direct democracy, democracy decreases with the passage of time, and as the organization grows in size or becomes more technically complex. In keeping with these expectations, Menachem Rosner and Arnold Tannenbaum (1987) found that age, size, and industrialization all made kibbutzim more likely to curtail democratic practices, and that kibbutzim belonging to the more ideologically committed Artzi Federation were more likely to retain them.

In addition to the expectation that these organizations lose their unique identities as they age or enlarge, another common theme in these literatures is that the organizational forms in question have more to fear from affluence than from poverty. For Rosabeth Kanter (1968), growing affluence weakens communes, because it undermines the asceticism that serves as an important source of solidarity. For Jaroslav Vanek (1977), accumulation of capital by producer cooperatives motivates them to minimize the number of members and to make increasing use of hired laborers. Raymond Russell and Robert Hanneman (1995) reported that worker cooperatives in Israel make increasing use of hired labor not only as the cooperatives age and enlarge, but also as they accumulate capital.

In addition to recommending that these organizations remain small, undifferentiated, and relatively poor, the literatures on democratic and communal organizations call attention to other potential influences on the readiness with which these organizations abandon their unique features. One influence is ideology. In the literature on kibbutzim, the effects of ideology have often been measured by comparing kibbutzim affiliated with the smaller and more ideologically coherent Artzi Federation to kibbutzim affiliated with the larger and more heterogeneous Takam; numerous studies have shown Artzi kibbutzim to be more faithful to kibbutz traditions than kibbutzim affiliated with Takam (Rosner and Tannenbaum 1987; Simons and Ingram 1997).

Finally, the literature on communes sees these communities as more likely to retain their structures to the extent they isolate themselves from contact with life outside the commune (Kanter 1968). For the kibbutzim, this view leads to the expectation that kibbutzim close to major cities will be more likely to introduce changes than will kibbutzim in distant rural areas (Ben-Ner 1987).

Kibbutzim as Organizations

Numerous previous studies have treated the kibbutzim as instances of democracy, cooperation, or communal life. Far fewer studies have viewed the kibbutzim simply as organizations. An important exception is Amitai Etzioni (1958, 1980), who identified the expanding organizational structures of the kibbutzim as the source of their increasing dependence on managerial elites. In the present work, we explore the relevance of three general organizational processes to the diffusion of changes among the kibbutzim. In many cases, we find general properties of the kibbutzim as organizations more relevant to the recent changes than any of the kibbutzim's idiosyncratic traits.

One important property that kibbutzim have in common with other organizations is "organizational inertia." According to Michael Hannan and John Freeman's (1984) theory of organizational inertia, all organizations become less likely to introduce changes of any kind, the older and larger the organization becomes. This expectation from organizational theory contrasts sharply with the literature on democratic and communal organizations, which sees such organizations as becoming more likely to lose their democratic and communal character as they age and enlarge. In addition to attaching importance to differences among organizations in their openness toward, or resistance to, change, the theory of organizational inertia emphasizes that change is difficult to make and often disruptive in its consequences (Greve 1999).

Like other organizations, the kibbutzim require resources, both human and material, in order to survive (Pfeffer and Salancik 1978). Christine Oliver's (1992) theory of "de-institutionalization" in organizations posits that organizations can afford to retain costly traditions when resources are plentiful, but may feel compelled to abandon them when resources become scarce. Resource scarcity also motivates organizations to adopt practices that increase their incomes or reduce their costs, even when those practices lack legitimacy in the eyes of relevant authorities (Kraatz and Zajac 1996). From this perspective, the kibbutzim most likely to introduce changes are those that have been experiencing the most severe shortages of financial and human resources. This constitutes another contrast with the literature on communal and democratic workplaces, in which these enterprises have often been accused of becoming more likely to abandon their alternative structures the more capital they accumulate or the more profitable they become (e.g., Kanter 1968; Russell and Hanneman 1995).

Also, like any other organization, each kibbutz belongs to a larger population of organizations that form part of the same organizational field (DiMaggio and Powell 1983), and with which they share a common organizational identity. Organizations gain stability and legitimacy by maintaining internally consistent practices that employ a common institutional logic (Friedland and Alford 1991) and that cohere around a recognized organizational archetype (Greenwood and Hinings 1993). Although institutionalized core identities serve as sources of resistance to change, membership in a common organizational field subjects organizations to the influence of examples set by other organizations in the same field (Ahmadjian and Robinson 2001). In the recent diffusion of changes among the kibbutzim, federations and government agencies have acted as enforcers of institutionalized core identities, while individual kibbutzim have imitated one another in ignoring the advice of both (Russell, Hanneman, and Getz 2006, 2010).

Dynamics of Change, 1990–2011

Overall, this work shows the literatures on democratic and communal organizations to be of only limited utility in explaining the incidence of recent changes among the kibbutzim. As expected, Artzi affiliation and distance from cities do make kibbutzim less likely to introduce changes, but the effects of kibbutz age, size, and economic condition are not what these works predict.

Theories that call attention to commonalities between kibbutzim and most or all other organizations, in contrast, are more relevant to these recent changes. Like most other organizations, kibbutzim are characterized by varying degrees of organizational inertia. This inertia makes organizations reluctant to change, and makes change difficult to implement, and disruptive when it occurs. As noted in Matthew Kraatz and Edward Zajac (1996), the motivation to introduce "illegitimate" changes arises not in prosperous and successful organizations, but in those in which performance pressures feed demand for change. Innovations arise not in strong organizations, but in weak ones, and then spread through imitation to other kibbutzim.

Plan of This Book

To understand how the kibbutzim have changed since 1990, and to appreciate how those innovations differed from those of prior years, it is necessary to begin by recounting what the kibbutzim were like in 1990, and how they came to be that way. Chapter 1 provides this background. It divides the history of the kibbutzim into two parts. The first part reviews the unique circumstances that gave birth to the kibbutzim, and that made them one of the most important forms of land settlement in Jewish Palestine in the first half of the twentieth century. The second part identifies changes in the kibbutzim between 1950 and 1985 that may have served as long-term causes of many later reforms; these changes include the industrialization of the kibbutzim, the growing use of hired labor, the shift from collective to private, family-centered consumption, and the aging of the kibbutz membership.

Chapter 2 addresses the crisis that the kibbutzim entered in 1985, and describes reforms that they adopted in response. It relies on surveys of all kibbutzim, conducted annually from 1990 through 2001, to identify which reforms were adopted by most kibbutzim in these years, and which were not. It documents the gradual diffusion of a large number of modest reforms, coupled with a general reluctance to make major changes. Most kibbutzim transferred authority for governing their economic ventures from the General Assembly to boards of directors, but refused to abolish the principle of rotating managers. Most kibbutzim gave members the right to take jobs outside the kibbutz, but the members' income earned on such outside employment continued to be paid to the kibbutz, not to the member. A growing portion of consumption expenditures, such as the costs of electricity and travel, became private rather than public, but most members' budgets continued to be based not on work but on need.

How kibbutzim made decisions to adopt or not to adopt these innovations is the subject of chapter 3. Previous studies of the diffusion of changes among organizations have relied on data that note only the presence or absence of innovations. In the University of Haifa's annual surveys of kibbutzim, respondents were given a long list of changes, and were asked to indicate for each change whether it had not been considered, had been rejected, was under discussion, had been decided, was in the process of being implemented, or was currently in use. These data show that few changes were adopted without first going through lengthy periods of discussion and/or of implementation. These deliberative and preparatory stages were not mere formalities, as the risks that an innovation would be abandoned were substantial at each stage, even after the innovation had been put into use.

Chapter 3 also examines the effects of organizational characteristics such as age, size, and economic condition on the readiness of kibbutzim to discuss, approve, implement, and retain innovations. The effects of organizational characteristics differ by stage. As the theory of Christine Oliver (1992) predicts, kibbutzim that are experiencing economic difficulty are more likely to consider innovations, and are less likely to drop innovations from consideration, once brought up. Once kibbutzim have decided to adopt an innovation, however, the economic condition of the kibbutz has no further effect on its subsequent implementation or retention. The size of a kibbutz, on the other hand, has no significant effect on the readiness of the kibbutz to consider innovations, but makes a kibbutz less likely to abandon innovations once they are being implemented or have been put into use. A declining membership is one of the few organizational characteristics with significant effects both early and late in the process, making kibbutzim both more likely to consider innovations, and less likely to abandon innovations once they have been decided upon. The most pervasive influence on the adoption of innovations is the proportion of all kibbutzim previously adopting the same innovation, making transitions toward use of innovations more likely at every stage of consideration and implementation.

Taken together, chapters 2 and 3 demonstrate that the kibbutzim were deeply ambivalent about change in the years from 1990 through 2001. Many more changes were proposed and discussed than were accepted, and many changes that had supposedly been decided upon were never or only briefly put into practice. Relatively innocuous proposals like having members pay for their own energy use successfully passed through all stages, but more radical proposals either were never brought up for discussion or were dropped in early stages of consideration. Kibbutzim that adopted more radical reforms, such as paying differential salaries to members, remained a small and daring minority until very late in this period.

Around 1995, a few kibbutzim such as Gesher Haziv and Naot Morde-chai developed a way to make payment of differential salaries more palat-able to kibbutz members. They adopted so-called safety-net budgets, in which members received differential, market-based salaries, but had their incomes taxed progressively to support a minimal standard of living and level of social services for all members. Between 1995 and 2011, more than 75 percent of Israel's 248 nonreligious kibbutzim adopted this safety-net budgetary system. During most of these years, another 5–15 percent of kib-butzim used some kind of mixed system of compensation.

Whereas the innovations that spread in the earlier period were mostly modest reforms, these new forms of compensation explicitly contradicted the traditional kibbutz principle of distribution on the basis of need. Given the radically transformative potential of these changes, chapter 4 focuses solely on them, examining the spread of the safety-net budget and of mixed systems of compensation during the years after 1995.

These analyses provide new opportunities to compare the relevance of the theories reviewed earlier. As theories of democratic and commu-nal organizations predict, adoption of new forms of compensation is more likely in kibbutzim that are older, closer to cities, and less attached to kib-butz ideology. As more general theories of organizations predict, transfor-mations are more likely in kibbutzim that are low in inertia, that suffer high levels of resource scarcity (Oliver 1992), and that witness similar transformations in other kibbutzim. Although both bodies of theory are applicable, it is the general theories of organizational change and of insti-tutionalized organizations that are more relevant to this transformation.

Whereas chapter 4 focuses on the introduction of differential com-pensation by individual kibbutzim, chapter 5 considers the implications of this innovation for the kibbutz federations and the Israeli government, and for the identity of the kibbutzim. In the 1990s, both the kibbutz federations and the Registrar of Cooperatives asserted that a kibbutz that paid differ-ential salaries to its members was no longer entitled to call itself a kibbutz, but they took no action to back up their threats to expel such kibbutzim. In 2002, the Israeli government asked a public committee chaired by Profes-sor Eliezar Ben-Rafael of Tel Aviv University to advise it regarding how to classify kibbutzim that introduced differential pay. Ben-Rafael's committee recommended in 2003 that kibbutzim that paid differential salaries should still be considered kibbutzim, but should be recognized as constituting kibbutzim of a new type, the renewing or renewed kibbutz (Ben-Rafael and Topel 2011; Manor 2004). By the year in which this recommendation was made, kibbutzim with safety-net budgets (111) already outnumbered kibbutzim that continued to base household budgets on need (107). The public committee's recommendations were later endorsed by the kibbutz movement and the government, and became law in October 2005.

Although Israeli law now describes any kibbutz that pays differential salaries as a renewed or renewing kibbutz, there is as yet no standardized vocabulary in Hebrew or English for referring to these kibbutzim. Annual reports of the kibbutz movement (Arbel 2004, 2005, 2006; Yoffe 2004) classify them as safety-net kibbutzim. Researchers at the Institute for Research of the Kibbutz at the University of Haifa (Palgi and Orchan 2007, 2009, 2011) designate them as "differential" kibbutzim. Kibbutz members now most frequently describe their kibbutz as having been "privatized" by these changes, and the Israeli media also follow this practice.

Whether the recent transformation of the kibbutzim will be remembered as the "privatization" of the kibbutzim or as the "renewal" of the kibbutzim thus remains to be seen. Although Israeli law now officially designates kibbutzim that pay differential salaries or have allocated property to individual members as renewed kibbutzim, most Israelis refer to such kibbutzim as privatized kibbutzim. We have titled the present work *The Renewal of the Kibbutz*, rather than *The Privatization of the Kibbutz*, because the changes described are, we believe, best viewed not as the dissolution or disappearance of the kibbutz, but as a change in the organizational identity of the kibbutzim. To make this case, we begin by describing the kibbutz as it looked when first invented, and show how much the identity of the kibbutz had already changed in the decades leading up to the recent wave of reforms.

1

Development of the Kibbutzim

In this chapter we describe the kibbutzim as they were at the opening of the period 1990 through 2010, and review how they came to assume that form. We divide relevant information about the nature and history of the kibbutzim into two parts. The first part relates the unique circumstances that gave birth to the kibbutzim, and that made them one of the most important forms of land settlement in Jewish Palestine in the first half of the twentieth century. The second part identifies changes that occurred in the kibbutzim between 1950 and 1985, changes that may serve as long-term causes of many later shifts. These include the industrialization of the kibbutzim, the growing use of hired labor, a shift from collective to private consumption, and the aging of the kibbutz members.

Origin and Spread, 1910–1950

In 1910, the kibbutz had just been invented, and it was not yet even known by that name. By 1950, however, the kibbutz had become one of Israel's best-known and most respected institutions. In most of the pre-state period of Jewish settlement in Palestine, and in the early years of the State of Israel, the kibbutzim were seen by Zionist leaders as important ways both to settle Jews on the land of Israel and to provide for the settlers' defense. The kibbutz also struck many idealistic young Jews in the Diaspora and in the Jewish settlement as the highest embodiment of their ideals and values. How did the kibbutzim come to play these roles during these years?

Roots of Labor Zionism

Before describing the birth of the first kibbutzim, it is necessary to acknowledge a few salient characteristics of the economic and social environment from which they were born. All but a few kibbutzim have been located on land owned by the Jewish National Fund (JNF). The JNF was founded in 1901 by the World Zionist Organization (WZO), created in 1898. Both the WZO and the JNF sought to settle Jews on the land of Israel.

Before the JNF made its first acquisitions, the WZO and its backers had already learned that making it possible for Jews to earn livings as farmers in Palestine would not be an easy task. The first wave of Jewish immigration to Palestine, known in Israeli history as the First Aliyah (1882–1903), had ended in failure. Zionist philanthropy in that period had sought to settle immigrants on individually owned farms. Many settlers turned out to have no idea how to farm or how to live in the Middle East. Thousands went back to their countries of origin in discouragement, or succumbed to disease. The small number who survived hired Arab laborers to work their farms, even while thousands of Jewish immigrants remained unemployed (Shafir 1989).

The decision to form the JNF reflected a shift to a new settlement policy by the WZO. The JNF would purchase land for settlement and retain title. It would lease plots of land to Jewish immigrants for specified periods; tenant farmers who were unsuccessful would be quickly replaced with other immigrants. In addition, the Zionist Settlement Office would henceforth be more selective about whom it helped to settle on the land; before immigrants would be allowed to farm on their own, they would need to spend one or more seasons on WZO-sponsored training farms.

The first would-be settlers who arrived to work on these farms were immigrants of the so-called Second Aliyah (1904–1914). These immigrants came from Russia or Austria-Hungary during the final years of those empires. It was a revolutionary era that fed the growth of nationalist and socialist movements of many kinds. Like other subject peoples of these empires, the Jews of the Second Aliyah wanted a nation-state of their own. Like their friends and relatives who made the Russian Revolutions of 1905 and 1917, they believed that a socialist utopia was about to be established all over the world, and they wanted to help make this happen.

Because the immigrants of the Second Aliyah were socialists as well as Zionists, they wanted to create a socialist economy, not a capitalist one, for Jews in Palestine, and they wanted to make their livings as members of the working class rather than of the bourgeoisie. The *chalutzim* ("pioneers") of this period wanted to be workers, not only to remain politically connected with the working class and its parties, but also to participate in what they saw as a redemptive value in manual work. They were inspired by authors like A. D. Gordon, who wrote that life in the Diaspora had distorted the development of Jews, forcing them into occupations that consisted primarily of mental work, and denying them opportunities to develop their bodies as well as their minds (Winer 1971). For these immigrants, to dirty their hands in the soil was not just a way to earn a living, but also a way to cleanse themselves of the effects of centuries of ghettoization.

Formation of Degania

It is conventional to say that the first kibbutz was Degania, and that the kibbutzim were born when Degania was formed in 1910. Although this statement is generally true, it contains some significant inaccuracies. Degania called itself not a *kibbutz*, but a *kvutzah*. Although both terms refer to communal settlements, a kvutzah is smaller, more homogeneous, and more selective than a kibbutz. Degania began with just ten men and two women, and some members believed that it should limit itself to a maximum of ten families (Gavron 2000).

The second inaccuracy in the conventional account is that, even if acknowledged to be an instance of a kvutzah rather than of a kibbutz, Degania in 1910 had not yet fully taken on the communal practices for which it would later be known. As Yitzhak Tabenkin later noted, "The kibbutz came prior to its idea. It had no preplan" (Kellerman 1993, 50). The founders of Degania were not self-consciously attempting to create a new form of organization.; until 1909, they had been working at the WZO's training farm at Kinneret, and told the WZO representative Arthur Ruppin that they found conditions there intolerable. The Russian agronomist whom the WZO had hired to run the farm was hiring Arab workers to do many tasks, and was treating Jewish immigrants like hired hands. Degania's founders asked

Ruppin for a chance to show that, working together as equals, they could compete successfully with Arab workers.

While they waited for Ruppin to allocate land to them, Degania's founders supported themselves by working as hired agricultural laborers near the coastal town of Hadera. It was there that they first organized themselves as a kvutzah, pooling their wages and living and eating together. When JNF-owned land became available in 1910, the kvutzah moved to Degania's current location, next to the Sea of Galilee, with no clear expectation that anyone else who came to work in Degania would become a member of the kvutzah. According to Daniel Gavron (2000, 24),

> The account books of the early years indicate that Degania was not a complete commune. The members of the Hadera Commune did function collectively. They were treated in the accounts as an individual unit, but the other members were credited for the days they worked and debited for the purchase of food and other items. So for the first decade or so it is true to describe Degania as a community containing a commune rather than a commune as such. It was only in 1923 that individual accounts disappeared from the Degania balance sheet, and the comprehensive communal structure was properly established.

Diffusion and Formalization of the Kvutzah

The experiment at Degania was quickly hailed as a success, both by Ruppin and by the many opinion makers among the Jewish immigrants who came to work there. In 1913, a second kvutzah was established, at Kinneret. Settlement activity was interrupted from 1914 to 1918 by World War I. Only two kvutzot, Ayelet Hashachar and Kfar Giladi, were established during the war years. Once immigration resumed in 1919, the number quickly rose to ten kvutzot in 1920, with a total population of 268 (Near 1992, 137).

In the years following World War I, jobs were scarce in Jewish Palestine, and the first opportunity many immigrants had to express their solidarity with the working class was to join a working-class political party like Achdut Haavodah or Hapoel Hatzair. The immigrants looked to these parties not only for political leadership, but also for help in obtaining jobs, food and housing, and medical care. In December 1920, the two parties merged their assistance efforts to form the General Federation of Jewish

Labor in Palestine, or Histadrut. Members of the kvutzot became members of the Histadrut by joining its Organization of Agricultural Laborers. In addition to the symbolic significance, membership in the Histadrut made kvutzot members eligible to receive medical care from clinics run by the Histadrut's medical service, the Kupat Cholim. It also meant that the Histadrut would support requests from the kvutzot for funds from the WZO and other Jewish philanthropies.

In 1922, a small group of members of Degania left the kvutzah to form Nahalal, the first instance of a more individualistic form of cooperative settlement known as a *moshav*. This group included Shmuel and Dvora Dayan and their young son Moshe, the future military leader. Whereas Degania's members ate their meals together and slept three or more to a room, the families that founded Nahalal wanted to sleep and eat in private households and to till their own fields. The role of the Nahalal cooperative would be confined to communal marketing, the provision of utilities like water and power, and limited forms of mutual support.

It was in the context of this development that Degania in 1923 stopped maintaining individual accounts for some workers, and instead made its entire labor force full members of the kvutzah. Thereafter, there would be a sharp contrast between the collectivism of the kvutzah and the individualism of the moshav.

The WZO's Jewish Settlement Office provided land and working capital for both kvutzot and moshavim, but, in a progress report published in 1926, Ruppin indicated that he preferred the kvutzah. One source of this preference was economic. As Ruppin put this point:

> *Group settlement requires a smaller initial investment than individual settlement* [italics Ruppin's]. A large house and a large stable are comparatively cheaper to construct than a corresponding number of separate houses and stables. The acquisition of the general equipment is also less expensive. . . . As an example: In an individual settlement each settler must own a cart, which he uses from time to time for purposes of transport, but which at other, probably longer periods, stands idle. Therefore, while a settlement of 60–80 individual colonists needs the same number of carts, a Kvutzah of similar size will probably only need 20–30 carts." (1926, 136)

After acknowledging such cost considerations, Ruppin added that, for the settlers, the decision to enter a kvutzah was more than "a question of mere utility and expediency":

> The hope that the Kvutzah is at the same time a better social system, . . . that it is another step in the social progress of man, this hope has imbued the settlers, especially those who have come from countries in Eastern Europe, which are at present in a state of ferment, with such energy that they were able to overcome difficulties to which they might otherwise have succumbed. They have come to look upon themselves, upon their agricultural work, . . . as work not only essential to the erection of a National Jewish Home in Palestine, but also closely connected with the social progress of all mankind. 'Man does not live from bread alone.' This is more than ever true in the case of the Palestinian settlers. (1926, 143)

From Kvutzah to Kibbutz

As Ruppin's comments suggest, the immigrants of the Third Aliyah (1919–1923) shared the socialist ideals of the Second Aliyah, but were more impatient to realize them. The Bolshevik revolution had occurred in 1917. If the new immigrants could not do something equally revolutionary in Palestine, they would go back to help build communism in Russia.

The members of a kvutzah practiced communism, but their communism was confined to a small elite. The kvutzot made a point of being highly selective, accepting as members only proven workers who shared their community's ideology. Members believed that, to retain their cohesion, the kvutzah needed to remain small.

In 1921, the model of organization that attracted the greatest interest among Jewish immigrants to Palestine was not the kvutzah but a newly formed organization, the *Gedud HaAvodah* ("labor battalion."). Like the members of a kvutzah, the members of the Gedud Haavodah would pool their money in a common purse. But the Gedud Haavodah, unlike a kvutzah, would be organized on a nationwide basis, enlisting as many workers as possible into a large and mobile labor army.

The Gedud and its allies argued that the kvutzah needed to be replaced by a new form of settlement, the kibbutz. Whereas the kvutzah was small and elitist, the kibbutz would be large and inclusive; whereas the kvutzah focused solely on farming, the kibbutz would engage in a wide range of agricultural and industrial pursuits.

Under the sponsorship of the Gedud, the first kibbutzim were established at Ein Harod and Tel Yosef in 1921, and others soon followed. Lacking the support of either the Histadrut or the political parties, the Gedud itself quickly fell apart, but the organizational form of the kibbutz survived as its enduring legacy. The kibbutzim quickly came to outnumber the kvutzot, and eventually gave their name to the entire population of collective agricultural settlements.

Federations, Parties, Youth Movements

The formation of the Gedud HaAvodah had been a challenge to the authority of the Histadrut, and to the political parties that had created it. To counter the appeal of Gedud, the Histadrut co-opted much of the Gedud's program. In 1924, it created its own alternative to the Gedud, which it called the *Chevrat Ovdim* ("workers' society"). Through the Chevrat Ovdim, the Histadrut would own and control many of the Jewish settlements' largest enterprises. Kibbutzim, moshavim, and urban worker cooperatives would also be considered by the Histadrut and its allies to be subsidiaries of the Chevrat Ovdim, although they were not directly under its control.

In this increasingly centralized political economy, the resources flowing to the kibbutzim would depend on the influence of their federations, and of the political parties with which these federations were affiliated. Kibbutz Meuchad, which means "United Kibbutz," was the federation whose aims were most similar to those of the Gedud HaAvodah. Formed in 1927, it advocated large kibbutzim, along with mutual responsibility among the kibbutzim. Kibbutz Meuchad was affiliated with the Labor Party; the Kibbutz Artzi Federation (whose name means "national kibbutz") was long affiliated with the more left-leaning Mapam.

For several decades, the kvutzot remained distinct from the kibbutzim, in a federation of their own, the *Chever HaKvutzot*. In 1951, a split within Kibbutz Meuchad led the kvutzot to join with kibbutzim departing from Meuchad in forming a new federation, the *Ichud HaKvutzot VeHaKibbutzim* ("union of kvutzot and kibbutzim"). By that year, the kvutzot were not much different from the kibbutzim in their structures or practices. In

1980, the Ichud and Kibbutz Meuchad merged to create the United Kibbutz Movement, known by the acronym Takam.

Of possibly even greater importance to the kibbutzim than the federations and political parties were the Zionist youth movements that supplied them with members. These movements were the first to spread the word in the Diaspora about the success of the kibbutzim. They also soon became very proficient at organizing prospective kibbutzniks into a nucleus, or *garin*, and in providing each garin with training and experience in farming and working together before their immigration to Palestine. After the Jewish communities of Europe were destroyed in the Holocaust, the role of the youth movements was diminished but not eliminated; they continued to operate in Israel and in many other countries. After Israel became independent, the Israeli army created a special branch, the Nahal, for young people who wished to use their military service to prepare for future life on a kibbutz.

Kibbutzim and Nation

Although the kvutzot and the kibbutzim were invented as ways to settle Jews on the land of Israel, they quickly acquired other functions. The most important of these was defense. The Jewish settlements in Palestine were being created on land that the JNF had legally purchased, but this did not prevent former Arab tenants from resenting the new Jewish owners. Shootings and skirmishes were frequent. The first self-defense force among the Jewish immigrants, *HaShomer* ("the watchman"), was closely allied with the communal settlements, and some of its members helped to found the kvutzah at Kfar Giladi. Later, when the Histadrut's Haganah took responsibility for the overall defense of Jewish Palestine, the kibbutz-based Palmach constituted its most elite units. When Israel became independent in 1948, the Haganah and Palmach became the core of the nation's army, and former kibbutz members contributed disproportionately to the army's officer corps and elite units for many years (Amir 1969).

Kibbutz members contributed to the creation and defense of Israel not only as individuals, but also as communities. As Arab resistance to the growth of Jewish settlements took an increasingly violent turn, in the 1920s and 1930s, the British began drafting contingency plans to partition Palestine between its Jewish and Arab populations. In 1937 the Peel

Commission recommended that, in the event of partition, demarcation lines should be based on which population was actually occupying each piece of land, not who had legal title. If all of the land owned by the Jewish National Fund was going to be included in the future Jewish state, it needed to be settled quickly, even in the midst of large and hostile Arab villages. To meet this need, a new kind of kibbutz began to be established in the 1930s and 1940s. Because these new "border kibbutzim" (Rayman 1981) were half settlements, half military outposts, they had a unique architecture, featuring heavy use of barbed wire and observation towers.

In addition to using the kibbutzim to defend and extend the area of Jewish settlement, Jewish leaders in the pre-state period also relied heavily on kibbutzim for help with immigrant absorption. By the time Israel's independence was declared, in May 1948, the kibbutz population had grown to represent 7.6 percent of Israel's Jewish population, its all-time peak percentage (Near 1997, 172).

In the War of Independence of 1948–1949, fighting reached the gates of many kibbutzim, including those like Degania that had not initially conceived of themselves as border kibbutzim. At Degania, one of two tanks that were stopped at the entrance stands as a permanent reminder of those times. Although the kibbutzim and many individual kibbutzniks emerged as heroes from the War of Independence, the new State of Israel would, in the future, take the lead in organizing the defense of the nation. The state would also increasingly rely on its own efforts rather than on those of the kibbutzim for immigrant absorption, as Tal Simons and Paul Ingram (2003) have shown. Whereas, until 1948, the kvutzot and the kibbutzim had been Jewish Palestine's most respected institutions, after Independence that status shifted to the army. With the army and the state then taking over the former role of the kibbutzim in nation building, the kibbutzim lost a major part of their reason for being, and they were left searching for new roles.

New Challenges, 1950–1985

In the 1950s and 1960s, the kibbutzim attracted increasing attention from international scholars as successful examples of utopian life (Spiro 1956) and as pioneers of important new forms of communal living and child-rearing (Bettleheim 1969). While the kibbutzim were being heaped with praise abroad, they were grappling, during these years, with growing challenges at home. Many of these new developments would throw into question the ability of the kibbutz way of life to outlive its founders.

Industrialization of the Kibbutzim

Although the idea that kibbutzim should engage in industry as well as agriculture goes back to the 1920s, most kibbutzim did not have sufficient resources to realize this ambition until the years after Independence. In 1940, only 815 kibbutz members, out of 6,079 members working in productive branches, worked in industry. By 1972, this number had grown to 10,591 out of 33,335 (Near 2007, 5). The kibbutzim experienced their first wave of industrialization during World War II, but most of the growth in kibbutz industries occurred in the 1960s and 1970s. The number of industrial ventures located on kibbutzim rose from 75 in 1956 and 100 in 1960 to 235 in 1973 (Barkai 1977, 110, 210, 212). By 1977, 75.2 percent of kibbutzim had at least one industrial enterprise, and 24.5 percent had two or more (Near 1997, 239–240).

By 1960, the proportion of kibbutz labor devoted to agriculture, forestry, and fishing had declined to 38.8 percent, but agriculture remained by far the largest single part of the kibbutz economy (Central Bureau of Statistics 1991). By 1990, the proportion of kibbutz labor taken up by agriculture had fallen to 22.9 percent, far below the proportion allocated to manufacturing, which had climbed, by that year, to 29.5 percent (Central Bureau of Statistics 1991). In the 1990s, the share of kibbutz labor going to agriculture continued to fall, to the point that it was eclipsed not only by manufacturing but also by the proportion of the kibbutz labor force providing services (Pavin 2007).

Adding industrial ventures to the economic activities of the kibbutzim allowed them to reach new highs in productivity, income, and population regularly for many decades (see table 1.1). Even while it clearly contributed to the growth of the kibbutzim, kibbutz industrialization also challenged kibbutz traditions in many ways. Two of the most important are its impact on the mix of skills required to run a kibbutz, and its impact on the use of hired labor.

The solidarity among the founders that led to the formation of Degania began as common resentment against an agronomist who thought that

TABLE 1.1

Number of Kibbutzim and Total Population of Kibbutzim, 1910–2010

Year	Kibbutzim	Population	Population per kibbutz
1910	1	11	11
1920	12	805	67
1930	29	3,900	134
1940	82	26,550	324
1950	214	67,550	316
1960	229	77,950	340
1970	229	85,100	372
1980	255	111,200	436
1990	270	125,100	463
2000	268	115,300	430
2010	265	140,900	532

Sources: Maron 1992 (as reported in Ben-Rafael 1997, 29); Pavin 2007, 5–6; Department of Economics 2012, 8.

his position and expertise entitled him to talk down to them. Degania's members were determined not to let the kvutzah split into classes of leaders and followers, or experts and managers. They quickly made it a practice to rotate leadership and other specialized positions among the members, so that no member would acquire power over the others by monopolizing the skills that such jobs require.

In rotating leadership positions, and in referring all important decisions to the General Assembly, the kibbutzim were practicing what Weber (1978) called "direct democracy." According to Weber, direct democracy requires four conditions: (1) the organization must be small enough for the members to get to know one another and to meet face-to-face; (2) administrative tasks must be simple and stable; (3) members must be equal in skill and social standing; and (4) members must receive training before they take on administrative tasks. As long as the kvutzot and kibbutzim consisted primarily of farmers engaged in agricultural pursuits together, these four conditions were being met. This may help to explain why the kibbutzim were hailed as providing successful examples of direct democracy for so long (Rosner and Cohen 1983). As the kibbutzim industrialized, however, all four conditions were undermined. The kibbutzim became larger and more differentiated workplaces, and they developed demand for a widening range of specialized skills. It became increasingly questionable whether kibbutzim would or should continue to rotate experienced managers out of their positions at the end of their terms.

The industrialization of the kibbutzim also threatened their ability to continue to minimize the use of hired labor. In designing its policy toward settlement, the WZO had been heavily influenced by the advice of Franz Oppenheimer (1896). Oppenheimer was skeptical about the economic prospects of cooperative workplaces in most branches of the economy, because he saw producer cooperatives as having a universal tendency to make increasing use of hired labor, gradually transforming themselves into capitalist firms. He saw agriculture as a field in which cooperatives could be competitive with enterprises that relied on hired hands, because the quality of agricultural labor is sensitive to the motivation of the workers. Cooperatives that initiated manufacturing ventures, on the other hand, would soon supplement and replace the labor of members with nonmembers. Oppenheimer's views were widely shared within the WZO and in the Histadrut, and the behavior of previous cooperatives in Israel's manufacturing sector appeared to confirm them (Preuss 1960; Russell 1995).

Hired Labor

One end or value that the WZO, the kibbutzniks, and the Histadrut all agreed on was the value of self-labor. The WZO knew that in the agricultural settlements of the First Aliyah, hired labor had quickly become non-Jewish labor. The kibbutz members wanted to share equally in farm labor, not to delegate that labor to others. In its role as guardian of the interests of the nonmember laborers, the Histadrut often reminded kibbutzim of their past commitments to provide opportunities for hired laborers to become members.

Although self-labor was a widely shared value, it did not come without costs. For individual kibbutzim, it meant foregoing the additional income that could be earned by adding the labor of hired workers to the efforts of members. For the new nation of Israel, it meant that the kibbutzim would provide fewer employment opportunities for new immigrants than they otherwise might have. This limitation soon became a source of tension between the kibbutzim and the new government. In 1950, Prime Minister David Ben-Gurion embarked on a campaign of publicly scolding the kibbutzim for their exclusiveness, declaring that he was now "ashamed" of his past association with the kibbutzim (Simons and Ingram 2003).

In the 1950s and 1960s, many kibbutzim responded to these temptations and pressures by increasing their use of hired laborers. The number of nonmembers employed on kibbutzim rose from 1,400 in 1951 to 7,500 in 1958 and 10,000 in 1965, by which time hired labor accounted for 19 percent of the total kibbutz labor force (Near 1997, 245). In kibbutz factories, as expected, the share of hired labor was even higher; in 1969 and 1970, it was reported to have reached 52 percent (Leviatan 1980).

In the 1970s, the kibbutz federations and the Kibbutz Industries Association (KIA) introduced a number of new initiatives designed to reduce the use of hired labor. The earliest kibbutz industrial ventures had clustered in branches like food processing and furniture making. It was now recognized that such labor-intensive activities were the most significant contributors to the growth of hired labor on the kibbutzim. In the 1970s and 1980s, the federations and the KIA encouraged kibbutzim to establish industrial ventures in more capital-intensive and highly automated pursuits, such as plastics, electronics, and precision tools. After Israel's victory in the Six Day War of 1967, increasing numbers of foreign visitors came to work on kibbutzim as unpaid volunteers (Mittelberg 1988); this, too, helped reduce the need for hired laborers. In response to these developments, the share of hired labor in kibbutz factories declined from 52 percent in 1969 and 1970 (Leviatan 1980) to 35 percent in 1980 (Kibbutz Industries Association 1983).

Studies by Tal Simons and Paul Ingram (1997) and by Menachem Rosner and Arnold S. Tannenbaum (1987) identified characteristics that made kibbutzim more or less likely to use hired labor during these decades. The research of Simons and Ingram (1997) covered the period from 1951 through 1965; Rosner and Tannenbaum (1987) relied on data collected from 1976 through 1979. Both studies reported that the more industrialized a kibbutz, the more likely it was to use hired labor.

Both studies also reported that the most important factor inhibiting the use of hired labor on kibbutzim during these decades was the influence of their federations. Kibbutzim affiliated with the Artzi Federation made significantly less use of hired labor than did other kibbutzim; those affiliated with the more permissive Ichud federation used significantly more hired labor. In 1980, the share of hired labor in kibbutz factories stood at 14 percent among the Artzi kibbutzim, 18 percent in Kibbutz Meuchad, and 50 percent in the kibbutzim of the Ichud. The Ichud figure, though high, was down from 77 percent in 1969 and 1970 (Kibbutz Industries Association, 1983).

From Collective to Private Consumption

The decades after Independence brought profound changes not only in how the kibbutzim earned their incomes, but also in how they spent them. In the first years of the kibbutzim, kibbutz members had little to share with each other but their poverty. The kibbutzniks' self-denying, ascetic values were well suited to the economic condition of the kibbutzim. Many of the collective practices of the kibbutzim were introduced not only for ideological reasons, but also as ways to economize on the scarce resources available to the kibbutz. As Arthur Ruppin noted, it was cheaper to operate a single communal kitchen than to have separate kitchens in every household. Communal houses for children, similarly, began from the fact that their parents' living quarters were not large enough to accommodate them.

In the years after Independence, as the standard of living in Israel and on the kibbutzim began to rise, the communal agricultural settlements started to be faced with new challenges, as private households assumed increasing importance. According to Henry Near (1997, 248), "In the early 1950s the area of a standard house for a kibbutz couple whose children slept in dormitories was 12 square metres." By the middle of the 1950s, "this had risen to 25–30 square metres for a veteran family, and by 1960, when the accepted level included a shower and toilet for each family, this had risen to 32, though the reality, particularly in the younger kibbutzim, was often very different. Ten years later the standard kibbutz dwelling included separate space for a bedroom and storage cupboards—52 square metres in all, while in kibbutzim where children slept in their parents' houses an extra 12 metres were added" (Near 1997, 248).

From the earliest years of the kibbutzim, members recognized that, as private households grew more comfortable and attractive, they would threaten the communal life of the kibbutz. An old slogan warns, "the koomkoom [tea kettle] will destroy the kibbutz" (Spiro 2004, 558). If members acquired the opportunity to prepare refreshments for themselves in private, kibbutzniks often asked, what would motivate them to eat in the communal dining hall, and what then would be left of the collective life of the kibbutz?

In addition to setting the kibbutzim on a path toward decommunalization, providing kibbutz members with private households also facilitated the development of inequality. At first, the kibbutzim resisted this, insisting that if one apartment obtained a radio, all members' apartments should receive radios; if one apartment acquired a television, all apartments should have televisions; and, eventually, if one apartment could have a color television, all apartments should have color televisions. Furniture was similarly standardized, by having the kibbutz provide it. Despite these egalitarian measures, the contents of kibbutz apartments became increasingly differentiated over time.

Growth in the private households of kibbutz members was matched by growth in members' personal incomes. In their early years, the kibbutzim took literally the principle of sharing income "from each according to ability, to each according to need." A kibbutz attempted to meet all its members' needs directly, purchasing items like clothes, toilet articles, and cigarettes collectively and leaving members no need to shop or carry cash. How many cigarettes or new shirts a member received, and how often members received opportunities to take vacations, within Israel or abroad, were governed by collective *norms*.

In the 1950s, some kibbutzim began to replace these systems of distribution according to norms with distribution according to *personal budgets*. Under the personal budget system, each member was credited with an allowance for each of several standard items of consumption—clothing, furniture, toilet articles, etc. The personal budget system was introduced by a few kibbutzim of the Chever HaKvutzot in 1946 and 1947. Although, at the time, this innovation was opposed by the leadership of the Chever HaKvutzot and all other federations, Near (1997, 296) notes, "The federative nature of this movement made it easier for the individual communities to make their own decisions on such matters, despite the opposition of the leaders." When Chever HaKvutzot joined with kibbutzim that had broken away from Kibbutz Meuchad in 1951 to form the Ichud, "the system spread through the whole of the new movement, and by 1962 had been adopted by all but two of its kibbutzim" (Near 1997, 296).

In the personal budget system, members were not permitted to shift money from one category to another. Money not spent on furniture or toilet articles could not be reallocated to clothes or recreation. Near reports, "This principle was gradually eroded, and in the course of the 1970s most of the kibbutzim of the Ihud adopted the principle of the inclusive budget, which was based on allocations for each group of items of expenditure, but allocated to each family as a lump sum."

The personal budget and the inclusive or comprehensive budget also gradually spread to the kibbutzim of Kibbutz Meuchad and Kibbutz Artzi, although, in the case of these federations, with their more centralized traditions, the pace of change was slower:

> In 1968 the personal budget was pronounced legitimate by the central committee of the Kibbutz Meuhad, and by the end of the 1970s, despite much initial opposition, most of its kibbutzim had adopted the inclusive budget. The Kibbutz Artzi was more successful than the other movements in resisting these tendencies, but despite strenuous efforts by the leadership to prevent the adoption of the personal budget, it gradually spread. The movement's 1975 conference tacitly accepted this system, but rejected the inclusive budget—even though twenty-six of the movement's seventy-eight settlements had adopted this practice, or something close to it. (Near 1997, 296)

As kibbutz households became larger and more comfortable, it became more feasible for children to sleep in their parents' apartments instead of in the communal children's houses. Near reports that "By the early 1920s, the practice of children sleeping in dormitories away from their parents had become standard in the great majority of kibbutzim," but notes that Degania and a few other older kibbutzim had always practiced "family sleeping." In the 1970s and 1980s, growing numbers of kibbutzim that had previously practiced communal childrearing switched to the family sleeping system. Once again, the change originated in the Chever HaKvutzot, and spread from it to the other movements. The first kibbutz to abandon communal childrearing was Gesher Haziv in 1949. According to Near (1997, 303), Gesher Haziv's family sleeping system was explicitly "modelled on that of Degania, and started a chain reaction within its kibbutz movement, the Ihud." This in turn led to pressures on the leadership of the movement to legitimize the system. "The Ihud establishment," writes Near, "firmly resisted this demand. But by 1960, by dint of exceptional persistence, a few Ihud kibbutzim had obtained permission to make the change, and were in the process of putting it into operation; and in 1967 the Ihud declared that both systems were legitimate" (1997, 303). Thereafter, "the example of the Ichud encouraged grassroots agitation to initiate a similar change in both the other movements. The Kibbutz Me'uhad followed suit in 1975, but the Kibbutz Artzi remained faithful to 'communal sleeping' until 1992" (Near 1997, 303).

Moving children to their parents' apartments obligated kibbutz members to spend even more money on their apartments. In a comparison of the portions of kibbutz consumption expenditures that went to collective consumption (communal dining hall, recreational facilities, etc.), or to individual consumption, in the years 1955 and 1965, Avner Ben-Ner (1987) had already observed an increase over time in the proportion of kibbutz expenditures made by individual households. Ben-Ner saw in this trend the gradual decommunalization of the kibbutz.

These changes in consumption on the kibbutzim were significant not only in themselves, but also in how they were made. Previous innovations in the kibbutzim, such as the growing defense role of the kibbutzim in the 1930s and 1940s, and the industrialization of the kibbutzim in the 1960s and 1970s, had been planned and coordinated by the leadership of their movements. Rising expenditures on personal consumption, in contrast, were being imposed on the leadership by the grassroots. Like the growing use of hired labor, the individuation of consumption was spreading from the less ideologically committed members, kibbutzim, and movements to the mainstream. With growing affluence, the kibbutzniks were losing their former asceticism and discipline. Many kibbutz members who received reparations payments from the German government or gifts from family members began to keep these sums in private bank accounts, even though such behavior remained against the rules (Near 1997; Rosenfeld 1957).

Amir Helman (1980) calls attention to one way in which the rising living standards of the kibbutzim continued to conform to tradition. After reviewing data on samples of kibbutzim in the years 1962–1971 and 1973–1974, Helman concluded that consumption expenditures on each kibbutz were less influenced by the income of the individual kibbutz than they were by the policies of its federation. In deciding how much of their incomes to spend on members, the kibbutzim were still following the guidance provided by their federations, rather than deciding on their own.

Changing Demography

Other important changes in the kibbutzim during the decades after Independence were demographic. The most significant was the reduction in the flow of new members sent by the Zionist youth movements of Europe and Israel. Such recruits knew what a kibbutz was, wanted to become a part of the kibbutz movement, and had already begun to work together as part of a garin. Immigrants who came to Israel in the 1950s and thereafter came from different countries, with different aspirations, and showed less interest in becoming members of kibbutzim.

With fewer immigrants entering the kibbutz population from the outside, the kibbutzniks relied increasingly on their own children as their most important source of new members. By 1986, the share of members in the Takam Federation originating from youth movements in Israel or abroad had fallen to 29.4 percent, while the portion born on the kibbutzim had risen to 31.4 percent (calculated from Maron 1998, 5).

Relying on the kibbutz-born to replenish the kibbutz involved two hazards. The first was that persons who had grown up on the kibbutz would be less committed to the kibbutz way of life than members who had deliberately chosen it. Early research on these so-called second-generation kibbutzniks indicated that they generally shared their parents' values (Rosner et al. 1990). Later, however, it was kibbutz-born members who took the lead in seeking higher standards of living, and more scope for nuclear families, on the kibbutzim (Ben-Rafael 1997, 164–165; Near 1997, 270).

The other risk in depending on the kibbutz-born for recruitment was that the children of the kibbutzim would prefer to pursue the range of alternative careers and lifestyles available outside the kibbutz. In the 1960s, sons and daughters of the kibbutzim were automatically enrolled as members when they graduated from high school, and 80 percent to 90 percent of each class returned to their kibbutzim upon completion of their army service (Near 1997, 269, 273). In the 1970s and 1980s, kibbutz-born young adults, like other young Israelis, began wanting to travel abroad and obtain university educations before finalizing their occupational choices. This both delayed the date of career decisions and increased the likelihood that kibbutz-born adults would choose to pursue specializations not available on the kibbutz.

By the 1980s, most kibbutzim considered themselves fortunate if half of their kibbutz-born children returned to live on the kibbutz as adults. The hope was that if each returning young adult brought a spouse who was not born on the kibbutz, the population of the kibbutz would be successfully renewed from one generation to the next. But it was already becoming apparent that more and more kibbutzim were failing to meet this target, and that their populations were beginning to decline.

While kibbutz-born young adults pondered whether or not to spend the rest of their lives on the kibbutz, the kibbutz population was becoming increasingly elderly. The proportion of the kibbutz population sixty-five years of age or older rose from only 1.4 percent in 1948 and 2.2 percent in 1961 to 4.2 percent in 1972 and 9.3 percent in 1983 (Maron [n.d.], 54). Where kibbutzim continued to grow and to prosper, their multigenerational societies and well-landscaped living quarters made them attractive places to spend one's retirement. But on kibbutzim whose populations were shrinking and whose incomes were uncertain, kibbutz members began to wonder who would maintain the kibbutz when current members became too old to work.

Institutionalization

Even while the influences just reviewed pushed the kibbutzim toward change, other influences served as powerful sources of resistance to change. Many of these had to do with the extent to which the kibbutzim had become institutionalized, both in the eyes of their members and federations, and in the eyes of the social movements and state in which they were embedded.

In sociology, it was customary for many decades to emphasize the differences between organizations and institutions. Whereas organizations originated in explicit acts of creation, institutions were products of long social evolution. Organizations pursued explicit goals; institutions served diffuse needs and interests. Organizations were small-scale, micro-societal phenomena; institutions were large-scale, macro-societal phenomena. Organizations could change rapidly; institutions changed slowly.

Since the classic work of Philip Selznick (1949, 1957) and Arthur Stinchcombe (1965), sociologists have become increasingly sensitive to ways in which the behavior of organizations can blur these neat distinctions. In Selznick's original formulation (1949), organizations become institutionalized to the extent that they come to be "infused with value" in the eyes of their participants. In Selznick's later work (1957), and in that of Stinchcombe (1965), it is this tendency of organizations to institutionalize their structures and practices that makes them increasingly resistant to change. For Michael Hannan and John Freeman (1984), similarly, it is this institutionalization of organizational structure that creates organizational "inertia."

Later theories of the institutionalization of organizational structures have shown that choices about structures and practices are not made by individual organizations in isolation. Organizations receive guidance from governments, universities, professional associations, media, consultants, and similar sources regarding the forms of behavior permissible, feasible, and/or desirable for them (Meyer and Rowan 1977; Scott 2008). Organizations may be especially responsive to examples set by other organizations that are part of the same field (DiMaggio and Powell 1983), that exemplify a common archetype (Greenwood and Hinings 1993), or that rely on a similar "institutional logic" (Friedland and Alford 1991).

Heather Haveman and Hayagreeva Rao (1997) refer to "the coevolution of institutions and organizations" to call attention to the many ways in which organizations and institutions interpenetrate and reinforce one another. They "propose that organizational form is tied to two distinct types of institutions that function at different levels of society. First, organizational forms make incarnate specific institutions—particular regulations, norms, and ideas that structure the actions of individuals and groups. Second, organizational forms are legitimated to the extent that they accord with general institutions—broadly accepted norms, values, and belief systems that constitute the master principles of society, such as truth, equality, and justice" (Haveman and Rao 1997, 1613–1614).

Israel's kibbutzim are institutionalized organizations, in many of these senses. Their structures and practices have been "infused with value" in the eyes of their participants since the day they were formed (Rosenfeld 1957; Spiro 1956). The birth of the kvutzot was an act of "institutional entrepreneurship" (Hardy and Maguire 2008) that "had no preplan" (Kellerman 1993, 50). As noted in Peter Berger and Thomas Luckmann (1967), what began as an improvised solution to practical problems quickly took on an objective character, since the kvutzot and the kibbutzim were both widely talked about and widely copied within years of their first appearance.

By linking the idealism of the Jewish immigrants with land and resources provided by Diaspora philanthropy, the kibbutz forged a potent alliance, and one that fit well into the political economy of Jewish Palestine. In the years of, first, the British Mandate and, later, the State of Israel, this relationship came to be embedded in and mediated by organizations and institutions operating on a larger scale. During the period of the Mandate, the most important of these influences were the political parties, the labor movement, and the kibbutz federations. Since Independence, another important institutional influence on the kibbutzim has been the State of Israel itself.

The formation of the State of Israel had mixed implications for the kibbutzim. In the years before statehood, public opinion in Jewish Palestine viewed the kibbutzim as the highest embodiment of widely shared Zionist and socialist values. For political leaders and philanthropists, the kibbutzim served as a favored means to settle Jews on the land, to absorb new immigrants, and to defend the borders of Jewish settlement. The formation of the State of Israel provided the kibbutzim with a new source of legitimation and patronage, but the new state displaced the kibbutzim as a central focus of Zionist and socialist aspirations. In a comparative study of cooperative movements in the midwestern United States during the late nineteenth and early twentieth centuries, Marc Schneiberg, Marissa King, and Thomas Smith (2008) predicted and found that socialist political parties would support cooperatives when those parties were weak and needed allies, but abandon cooperatives when the parties became strong enough to get along without cooperative allies. In Israel, similarly, Prime Minister David Ben-Gurion and many other socialist leaders supported the kibbutzim and other cooperatives during the pre-state period, but shifted their attention away once the new state came under their direct control (Ingram and Simons 2000; Simons and Ingram 2003).

Although, indeed, Ben-Gurion and some other socialist leaders distanced themselves from the kibbutzim in the years after statehood, kibbutz members remained integral parts of several Israeli political parties for many years. In the first two decades after Independence, kibbutz members typically filled one-sixth or more of the seats in the Knesset, and made up a quarter or more of many cabinets (Near 1997, 258–259). Even though kibbutz members rarely filled the highest government posts, they often served as ministers of agriculture, education, health, or transport (Near 1997, 260). Eliezer Ben-Rafael notes, "These political strongholds . . . for long offered a way of obtaining privileges and special attention; they certainly helped the kibbutzim economically, not to speak of the public authority and social status they brought along" (Ben-Rafael 1997, 38). Near observes, similarly, "Representatives of the kibbutz movements in the parties, the government, and the Histadrut served as an interest group for their own economic sector, believing firmly that its interests were identical with those of the country as a whole" (Near 1997, 260).

Although kibbutz members remained part of every Israeli government until the victory of Likud in 1977, even before this sea change in Israeli politics, as Near writes, "the years between 1954 and 1977 saw a marked decline in the influence of the kibbutz movements in the Israeli political system" (Near 1997, 256). Near attributes this political decline in part to a decline in the status of the kibbutz, as kibbutz members came to be perceived less as heroes and more as an interest group, and in part to changes in how political parties chose candidates for offices, with rural voters and party officials losing influence to urban voters.

While the kibbutzim had entered a period of political decline even before 1977, Ben-Rafael writes, "The rise to power of the right-wing Likud party in 1977 . . . amounted to no less than an earthquake for the kibbutz movement. It dislodged the federations from the longstanding positions—in the Ministries of Agriculture, Education, or Commerce and Industry, and even the Ministry of Defense—where their presence had been strong through representatives and institutionalized lobbying. Moreover, in Parliament itself, the representation of the kibbutzniks was drastically cut, while they were now totally absent from the government, where they customarily had held one or two positions under the Labor rule" (Ben-Rafael 1997, 38).

Although the State of Israel has provided far less support for the kibbutzim in recent decades than it did in earlier years, there are two important ways in which it has continued to contribute to the institutionalization of the kibbutzim. First, through its Land Authority, the State of Israel took over from the World Zionist Organization (WZO) the stewardship of land owned by the Jewish National Fund (JNF). In this capacity, the state continued to allocate land for the formation of new kibbutzim, and retained the policy of leasing the land rather than giving or selling it to the founders. If kibbutz members had been free to buy and sell farms among one another or with outsiders, the kibbutzim would likely not have been so long-lived. But such sales have not happened, because the State of Israel through its Land Authority has remained the ultimate landlord.

The second important way that the State of Israel has contributed to the institutionalization of the kibbutzim lies in its having taken over from the British Mandate the office of the Registrar of Cooperatives. During the Mandate, the Registrar of Cooperatives maintained official lists of cooperatives of various types, including kibbutzim, moshavim, and cooperatives engaged in production, transportation, or services (Russell 1995). Registration as a cooperative entitled an organization to have government-required audits performed by an audit union made up of cooperatives of the same type; the State of Israel retained this practice.

For the government to maintain such lists of cooperatives by types, it needs to have official definitions of each type. This has put the Israeli government in the position of de facto enforcer of organizational identities among Israeli cooperatives. The Registrar of Cooperatives publishes and periodically updates a set of *Cooperative Societies Regulations.* In 1995 these rules defined a kibbutz as "a cooperative society that is a separate settlement, organized on the basis of collective ownership of assets, self-employment, equality and cooperation in production, consumption and education." By including this definition in its laws, the State of Israel both legitimates and institutionalizes the unique identity of the kibbutz. Implicitly, this regulatory relationship also gives the Registrar of Cooperatives responsibility for policing that identity. Because the State of Israel acknowledges the kibbutzim and other cooperatives, but has little need or use for them, the Registrar of Cooperatives has not, however, been active or consistent in making sure that they adhere to the official definitions.

Threats from the Registrar of Cooperatives to expel aberrant cooperatives having been expressed only intermittently, most day-to-day work of safeguarding the identity of the kibbutzim has been performed by the federations. In the 1970s and 1980s, it was the kibbutz federations and the closely allied Kibbutz Industries Association (KIA) that led efforts to minimize the use of hired labor in kibbutzim.

In the 1970s, the federations also encouraged member kibbutzim to protect themselves against changes that might undermine their identities, by committing their collective structures to writing. Most kibbutzim had been organized with a minimum of documentation. In the 1970s, the kibbutz movement established a legal department, which advised the federations that each kibbutz needed to adopt a charter or set of bylaws (in Hebrew, *takanon*) and file it with the Registrar of Cooperatives. The federations circulated model bylaws, and most kibbutzim adopted them with few, if any, changes. In addition to repeating the definition of a kibbutz contained in the Registrar's Cooperative Societies Regulations, these documents declared that "the kibbutz is entitled to receive ownership and possession of all property of the member," and that "the kibbutz property is not distributable among its members, neither during its existence nor upon its liquidation" (Yassour 1977, 331, 333). Kibbutz bylaws and any subsequent amendments required the consent of three-quarters of the membership, and also needed to be approved by the kibbutz movement.

Recent studies of institutionalized organizations have emphasized that institutional processes affecting organizations take place at multiple levels. This is clearly true of the kibbutzim. The unique practices and identity of the kibbutzim were institutionalized first of all in the hearts and minds of their individual members, where they continued to be "infused with value." At the organizational level, all of the kibbutzim were acquiring various forms of inertia, including bylaws that would make their structures difficult to amend. At the levels of organizational field and of the state, the kibbutz federations and the Israeli government had come to promote shared understandings about the identity of the kibbutz.

Changing Identity of the Kibbutzim

It is clear that the kibbutzim were already changing in important ways long before an economic and demographic crisis hit them in 1985. The communal childrearing practices for which the kibbutzim were famous had already been abandoned. The kibbutzim of the 1980s were already very different from the kvutzot of the pioneers, and they were continuing to undergo further change. The kibbutzim were becoming more differentiated, more individuated, and more family-centered with each passing year. Observers like Avner Ben-Ner (1987) and Erik Cohen (1983) reported that the kibbutzim were already losing their communal character, and gradually transforming themselves into organizations of a different type.

Despite these signs of decommunalization, the kibbutzim in the 1980s still retained most of the communal and democratic practices that they were known for. The kibbutzim did not pay salaries to members, and continued to meet members' basic needs collectively, feeding them in communal dining halls, and providing them with housing, medical care, and educations for their children. All important decisions continued to be made by the General Assembly of all the members. The kibbutzim continued to decide where each member worked. Experienced managers continued to be rotated out of their positions at the end of fixed terms.

The fidelity of the kibbutzim to their collectivist and egalitarian traditions was not accidental; the stability of these practices was supported by institutional processes operating at every level of Israeli society. Within individual kibbutzim, most members continued to believe in the value of these practices, and they had now codified their most important collective features in their charters. The kibbutz federations worked to keep departures from cooperative ideals, such as the use of hired labor, within tolerable limits. Israel's Land Authority and Registrar of Cooperatives helped to constrain the profit-seeking and commercialism that had undermined cooperation and communalism in other contexts. The social movements and political parties with which the kibbutzim were affiliated reinforced their shared values, and celebrated the unique identity and practices of the kibbutzim.

Although this array of forces helping to institutionalize the identity of the kibbutzim is impressive, it would be a mistake to exaggerate their power. As the persistent use of hired labor indicates, there has never been a perfect fit between the way the kibbutzim are defined and described on paper, and the way they actually behave. From the formation of the first kvutzah to the end of collective childrearing, the kibbutzim have continued to validate Yitzhak Tabenkin's observation that "the kibbutz came prior to its idea" (Kellerman 1993, 50). The federations have been successful in having the unique structures and practices of the kibbutzim codified in Israel's Law of Cooperatives and in the charters of individual kibbutzim, but in these instances their achievement has been to institutionalize the status quo on the kibbutzim rather than to shape it. The abandonment of collective childrearing shows that, when kibbutz members wish to make a change not barred by national law or the kibbutz charters, the federations have only limited ability to prevent their doing so.

2

From Crisis to Reform, 1985-2001

By the 1980s, Israel's kibbutzim differed in many ways from what they had been in the pre-state period. Most kibbutz members now worked outside of agriculture, in increasingly diverse tasks. They now slept in family-based households. The trees and plants growing on many kibbutzim were now mature and well-tended, giving their grounds a park-like atmosphere. Since the 1970s, visitors were reporting that the overall look of the kibbutzim was "becoming bourgeois" (Near 1997, 249).

Despite these outward signs of affluence and embourgeoisement, the kibbutzim in the 1980s still retained most of the communal and democratic structural features and practices for which they were famous. All important decisions continued to be made by the General Assembly of all the members. Managers continued to be rotated out of positions at the end of their terms. The kibbutzim continued to decide where each member worked, and continued to meet members' basic needs collectively, feeding them in communal dining halls, and providing them with housing, medical care, and education for the children. The supplemental incomes that members received in addition to these collective goods continued to be based not on work but on need.

By the end of the 1980s, all of these previously unchallenged practices would begin to be questioned. But before these traditions came under assault, the kibbutzim would be struck by a series of shocks. In the early 1980s, the government's economic policies had been expansionary, making credit available on easy terms. These policies fueled inflation, making it even easier to pay off old loans and obtain new ones. During this period, the kibbutzim, like most other Israeli enterprises, became heavy borrowers. In 1985, the Israeli government suddenly shifted its economic policy from inflationary to deflationary, to stabilize the declining value of the currency. As part of the government's emergency price stabilization plan, all debt in Israel would henceforth be indexed to the rate of inflation. The kibbutzim, like other Israeli borrowers, saw their debts grow larger with each increase in the rate of inflation just as their ability to repay those debts was declining, because the national economy had gone into a recession.

Businesses throughout the Israeli economy found themselves caught between upwardly spiraling debts and downwardly spiraling incomes. Many became bankrupt, including the nation's largest banks. Increasing numbers of individual kibbutzim found themselves unable to pay their debts. Because the kibbutzim were guarantors of each other's debts, the kibbutz movement as a whole fell into bankruptcy.

The account given so far portrays the kibbutzim as passive victims of macroeconomic forces beyond their control. Defenders of kibbutz traditions remained loyal to such accounts well into the 1990s. But growing numbers of critics pointed to many ways in which the kibbutzim had brought their economic problems on themselves. Many investments made in the early 1980s appeared with hindsight to have been unwise. These included both risky economic ventures that later went bad, and the high proportion of capital resources used to build the larger living quarters required by family sleeping.

The first and loudest voice to blame the kibbutzim for their own problems was the Likud government. Within Israel, the Likud government, which had held or shared power since 1977, represented the victory of pro-business parties over labor parties, and of Israelis with roots in Asia or North Africa over those with roots in Europe. Internationally, the Likud leaders were ideological allies of Margaret Thatcher and Ronald Reagan, and shared their agenda. The Likud leaders were quick to label the economic difficulties of the kibbutzim as additional examples of the failure of socialism. Like their allies abroad, they prescribed privatization as the only solution to troubled economies.

Critics outside the kibbutz movement were soon joined by voices within. In kibbutz managerial training centers like the Ruppin Institute, and in the Takam Federation's archive and publications center at Yad Tabenkin, researchers began to identify practices of the kibbutzim that might have contributed to the recent poor performance of their economic ventures. Critics like Reuven Shapira (1990), for example, argued that the rotation of managers in kibbutz factories was depriving those enterprises of the services of their most skilled and successful leaders. For Gideon Kressel (1991), the problem was that the collective ownership and decision-making practices of the kibbutz left managers insufficiently accountable for their errors.

As kibbutz members asked each other who and what had caused their current problems, and what they needed to do to resolve these issues, many began to lose confidence that the kibbutz remained viable in the contemporary Israeli economy. Many kibbutz members and adult children of members left to pursue more attractive opportunities elsewhere. This led the kibbutzim's economic crisis to be compounded by a demographic crisis.

In 1985, the total number of members, children of members, and other residents living on kibbutzim stood at 125,200 (Maron 1994). Spread over 268 kibbutzim, this represented an average of 467 residents per kibbutz. Both figures were all-time highs at the time, and substantially higher than a mere five years before, in 1980 (see table 1.1). Over the five years from 1986 through 1990, however, more adults departed from kibbutzim each year than became new members.

Using data first assembled by Joseph Lanir (1993), Eliezer Ben-Rafael (1997) reviews counts of the number of adults entering and leaving the kibbutzim in each year from 1981 through 1990. In the early 1980s, the number of residents leaving each year was closely balanced by the number of new members. In the latter half of the decade, however, the balance turned sharply negative, with the number leaving exceeding the number joining by 2000–3000 per year. That represents a loss of 6–10 residents per year per kibbutz, or 35 over the five years. Only natural population increase (the excess of births over deaths) allowed the total population of the kibbutzim to remain as high in 1990 as it had been in 1985 (Ben-Rafael 1997, 28–30).

Stanley Maron (1991) examines the impact of departures of members and children of members on the changing age structure of the kibbutzim during these years. Between 1983 and 1986, the kibbutzim were successfully attracting and retaining adults with teen-age or younger children. Between 1986 and 1989, the number of kibbutz residents aged 25–34 fell by 11.4 percent, and the number of children 0–4 years of age fell by 6.6 percent. The number of kibbutz members 65 or more years of age, in the meantime, grew steadily in both periods.

The perception that the kibbutzim were failing to appeal to the younger generation, and that they were losing many of their most promising workers, lent urgency to calls for reform. By the late 1980s, reforms were being urged by voices both outside and inside the movement. Discussions about which reforms the kibbutzim should or should not adopt quickly became ideologically charged and hotly contested, both within individual kibbutzim and in the kibbutz federations.

In 1988, Yehuda Harel issued a call for a "new kibbutz," while serving as head of the Takam Federation's archive and publication center at Yad Tabenkin (Harel 1988). Harel's new kibbutz was to be a much freer, more individualistic, and more economically rational entity than the previous one. Each factory or other enterprise would be autonomous from the kibbutz General Assembly and would have control over its own labor and capital inputs. The centralized distribution of goods would almost completely disappear. The incomes provided to members by the kibbutz would continue to be based on need rather than work, but members would be free to spend those allotments however and wherever they wished.

Harel's views were quickly taken up by other influential spokespersons, but they also aroused strong opposition. Leaders of the major kibbutz federations gave the new kibbutz a cold reception, and influential theorists like Menachem Rosner (1988) denounced it. Other faculty at Yad Tabenkin were so offended by Harel's new-kibbutz model, that he was forced to give up his position. Harel appealed to the rank and file of the United Kibbutz Movement for support, but was soundly defeated in a bid to become the leader of Takam.

In negotiations with the government over the terms for repayment of their debts, the kibbutz federations in 1989 formally committed their member kibbutzim to introduce reforms, but left each kibbutz free to determine which reforms it would or would not adopt. Because Harel's new-kibbutz model had produced such a hostile response, the kibbutzim received little guidance from it, and instead embarked on this journey without any road map. The price that Harel had paid served as a warning that kibbutz members should not wander far from the status quo in recommending reforms.

In the early 1990s, members of many kibbutzim were scandalized by a proposal from Kibbutz Ein Zivan to begin paying differential, market-based salaries to its members. The kibbutz federations threatened to expel from the movement any kibbutz that adopted such a reform. They made it clear that they would permit changes that were consistent with the historic identity and legal definition of the kibbutzim, but would not accept changes that they viewed as inconsistent.

To help make decisions about changes, many kibbutzim set up "innovation teams" with the assistance of their federations, to identify reforms that looked especially appropriate (Near 1997, 352). Menachem Rosner and Shlomo Getz note that such committees were unique in kibbutz history because "These bodies are not concerned with solving problems as they arise, as in the past, but with suggesting and initiating changes to the kibbutz" (1994, 42). In making decisions about which changes to adopt, many kibbutzim sought advice from their federations or from professional consultants.

Despite these facilitators, many kibbutzim found themselves deeply divided between reformers and traditionalists, and uncertain about what to do next (Ben-Rafael 1997; Palgi 1994, 2002). Reforms tended to be backed by "technocrats," who would seek a freer hand in management, and by younger, kibbutz-born or Israeli-born members, who would seek lifestyles more similar to those of Israelis outside the kibbutzim (Topel 2005). Traditional kibbutz values and practices tended to be defended by older members and by members born outside Israel (Ben-Rafael 1997).

Diffusion of Changes, 1990–2001

In the late 1980s, increasingly loud voices both outside and within the kibbutz movement were calling on the kibbutzim to adopt reforms. In 1989, the kibbutz federations formally committed their members to introduce innovations designed to make their economic activities more profitable and productive; this was part of the agreement by which they emerged from bankruptcy (Ben-Rafael 1997). Which reforms would or would not be adopted on each kibbutz was left up to that kibbutz. Many kibbutzim set up special committees to make recommendations regarding changes for their own kibbutzim; others asked existing committees to perform this function.

Having promised their creditors that the kibbutzim would introduce reforms, the kibbutz federations needed a way to document compliance. They requested the University of Haifa's Institute for Research of the Kibbutz and the Cooperative Idea to conduct annual surveys: every year from 1990 through 2001, the Institute surveyed all kibbutzim about reforms under consideration at the time (Getz 1994, 1998a). In motivating kibbutzim to respond to its survey, the Institute had the benefit of being able to say that the survey was cosponsored by the kibbutz federations. In 1990, the survey was mailed to 254 nonreligious kibbutzim, and 135 responses were received, a response rate of 53 percent. In later years, as shown in table 2.1, 200 or more kibbutzim responded to the survey in almost every year, producing response rates of nearly 80 percent or better each year.

As new reforms came under discussion, they were added to these annual surveys, and reforms that did not catch on or that were almost universally adopted were dropped. During the twelve years from 1990 through

TABLE 2.1.

Kibbutzim Responding to Surveys,
1990–2001

Year	Number responding
1990	135
1991	210
1992	191
1993	203
1994	204
1995	196
1996	221
1997	225
1998	225
1999	203
2000	213
2001	207

2001, a total of seventy-five changes were included in one or more of the surveys. This chapter presents data on the incidence of all seventy-five.

The changes adopted by one or more kibbutzim during this period were very diverse. Some were intended to strengthen the traditional kibbutz, by making it more efficient, more productive, or more attractive to current and future members. Others were intended to implement one or more visions of the "new kibbutz" (Harel 1988).

Changes considered by the kibbutzim during this period can be sorted into three major groups: changes in the way kibbutzim would make decisions and govern their economic ventures; proposals to increase the role of non-members in the kibbutz economy and community; and changes in the relationship between kibbutzim and their individual members. This last group includes proposals to expand the rights or entitlements of members and their children, changes that privatized consumption and communal services, and proposals to make increased use of material incentives or to transfer ownership of homes or other assets from kibbutzim to their individual members.

Changes in Decision Making

Menachem Rosner and others have often noted (e.g., Rosner and Blasi 1985; Rosner and Cohen 1983) that the traditional kibbutz constitutes a rare instance of Max Weber's concept of "direct democracy." In this model, leadership positions are rotated, and all major decisions are made by an assembly of the members. In the years after 1985, many critics blamed the economic difficulties of the kibbutzim on these practices, and urged the kibbutzim to transfer control of their economic ventures from the General Assembly to specialized experts.

The changes in decision making that were being adopted by at least some kibbutzim in the years between 1990 and 2001 fall into three major groups (table 2.2): delegation of kibbutz-wide decisions to committees or individuals; establishment of boards of directors; and differentiation and rationalization of sources of income. In all three categories, most proposals received at best only a mixed reception, with few changes gaining the acceptance of half or more kibbutzim during this period.

In the first group, two reforms sought to create new committees to exercise authority previously exercised by the General Assembly. The use of representative councils rose from 3.8 percent of responding kibbutzim

TABLE 2.2.

Rationalization of Management and Decision Making (Percentage of

	1990	1991	1992
Delegation and Specialization in Decision Making			
Representative council	3.8	12.8	19.1
Internal control committee	0.4	0.8	1.2
Replace committees by office holders	2.4	5.8	10.4
Abolishing the rotation of managers	4.4	6.5	11.2
Boards of Directors			
Board of directors in industry	10.7	22.5	38.2
Board of directors in agriculture	3.2	4.8	7.9
Board of directors			
Board of directors for the community			
Rationalization of Sources of Income			
Economic branches as profit centers	13.3	7.4	17.1
Separating the economy from the community	5.0	3.2	7.4
Incorporation of branches			
Shadow wages	4.8	3.5	7.1
Human resources division			
Members working outside as a branch			

in 1990 to 28.0 percent in 1998, before declining to 23.4 percent in 2001. Internal control committees—committees with the purpose of limiting the power of managers and other committees—were reported to be in use in only one kibbutz in 1990, but the proportion of kibbutzim that had adopted this reform had risen to 32.2 percent in 2001.

Two proposed reforms sought to delegate the authority of the General Assembly, not to committees, but to individuals. A policy of replacing committees with office holders had been embraced by 2.4 percent of responding kibbutzim in 1990. In 1999, the last year in which this reform was asked about, the figure had risen to 20.5 percent. Abolishing the rotation of managers had

Responding Kibbutzim Reporting Adoption of Innovations by Year)

1993	1994	1995	1996	1997	1998	1999	2000	2001
22.5	25.3	25.2	26.3	27.6	28.0	24.9	26.2	23.4
1.6	2.9	3.8	7.4	11.1	15.8	15.0	23.8	32.2
10.8	12.8	15.1	13.5	16.2	16.7	20.5		
12.1	15.2	21.9	25.8	23.9	26.3	25.9	31.9	
43.5	53.2	58.7	61.6	64.0	68.7	75.1	65.1	60.2
10.2	13.9	19.0	22.5	29.1	32.3	34.3	19.4	19.1
			10.8	15.6	18.9	16.4	21.3	14.9
						12.5		
13.6	16.4	13.9	16.2	28.0	32.3	32.9	49.1	57.2
9.5	10.9	14.2	13.9	18.8	23.0	33.5	48.6	57.4
							33.5	43.2
7.0	7.4	8.9	13.7	21.2	31.9	42.7	49.7	55.9
23.1	23.4	28.2	26.0	35.5	49.8	61.8	64.4	73.9
						42.8	29.4	41.8

been adopted by 4.4 percent of responding kibbutzim in 1990, 31.9 percent in 2000. In practice, many more kibbutzim were allowing managers to serve longer terms, honoring the tradition of rotating managers only in principle.

One of the most widely adopted reforms of the 1990s was the creation of independent boards of directors to govern kibbutz industrial ventures. Such boards were typically made up of knowledgeable members of the kibbutz, members of other kibbutzim with experience in similar ventures, and individuals with expertise gained in the private sector. The use of this practice was reported by 10.7 percent of responding kibbutzim in 1990 but had risen to 75.1 percent in 1999. Boards of directors for agricultural ventures was a reform less widely adopted, reaching its highest penetration at 34.3 percent in 1999 and falling to 19.1 percent in 2001. Boards of directors have also been proposed for the community or for the kibbutz as a whole, but this idea has been less widely adopted.

The last set of proposals for changing the management of the kibbutzim included innovations in accounting and in structure. As Martin Buber noted (1958), a traditional kibbutz is neither a producers' cooperative nor a consumers' cooperative, but rather a "whole cooperative" uniting production with consumption. Three reforms promoted separation of kibbutz economic ventures from the community and from each other. Separating the economy from the community had been adopted by 5.0 percent of responding kibbutzim in 1990, rising to 23.0 percent in 1998. Treating economic branches as profit centers had been adopted by 13.3 percent in 1990 and 32.9 percent in 1998. Incorporation of branches entered the survey in 2000, by which time this reform had been adopted by 33.5 percent of responding kibbutzim; a year later, this proportion had risen to 43.2 percent.

The final three reforms listed on table 2.2 addressed the way kibbutzim accounted for and coordinated the labor of their members. In a traditional kibbutz, members received a *budget* from the kibbutz that was based on their needs, not a *wage* earned through their work. Still, although individual kibbutz members did not receive wages, supporting them and their families did create certain costs. To encourage kibbutz ventures to economize on scarce resources, all kibbutzim treated the cost of the labor of members associated with each venture as an expense of that venture; traditionally, the cost of a member's labor had been calculated on the basis of average consumption expenses. In kibbutzim that switched to systems of so-called shadow wages, the cost of a member's labor was calculated on the basis of the general labor market; the shadow wages assigned to members were unequal, but were not made public and had no impact on members' incomes. The proportion of kibbutzim reporting that they calculated such differential shadow wages rose from 4.8 percent in 1990 to 55.9 percent in 2001.

With increasing numbers of members working outside the kibbutz, and of nonmembers working within it, the percentage of kibbutzim reporting that they had established human resource divisions climbed from 23.1 percent in 1993 to 73.9 percent in 2001. Treating members who worked outside the kibbutz as a distinct economic branch was being practiced by

42.8 percent of responding kibbutzim when this question was added to the survey in 1999, and by 41.8 percent in 2001.

This record of mixed and partial success for changes involving decision making is consistent with the findings of a recent study by Menachem Topel (2005) that investigated the internal politics of 118 events of change in thirty-four kibbutzim. According to Topel, proposals to change the economic structure of a kibbutz and its methods of decision making are initiated by "the technocrat," whom Topel defines as "a technical expert who has a higher education" and who "holds a managerial position in an organization in which he coordinates complex systems" (2005, ii). Topel notes: "Although the technocrats . . . possess a great deal of influence, which enables them to implement limited changes without any public discussion, many proposals are not accepted or implemented" (2005, iv–v). Regarding the reluctance of the members to delegate more decision-making authority to the managers, Topel adds, "The limitations that other people place on the technocrats suggest that they also have a certain degree of influence and that the technocrats have to take into consideration the public at large" (2005, iv).

Nonmembers in Production and Services

Although proposals to rationalize the management of the kibbutzim received only a mixed reception during this period, many other innovations were much more readily adopted. One such set of changes brought kibbutz members into much more frequent contact with nonmembers than they had ever known. Kibbutzim had traditionally sought to minimize the role of nonmembers in their economies; in the socialist political economies of Jewish Palestine and, later, Israel, employment of nonmembers was viewed as exploitative, and as a sign of the transformation of a cooperative enterprise into a capitalist one. Living in distinct communities and operating their own educational institutions helped the kibbutzim maintain their values and transmit these to their children. (The literature on utopian communities suggests that preserving such unique value systems becomes more difficult, the more contact community members have with outsiders [Kanter 1968]).

In the decades before the 1990s, the role of nonmembers in the kibbutz labor force rose in some periods and fell in others, depending on the policies of the federations, and the economic circumstances of the kibbutzim (Simons and Ingram 1997). It increased in the 1960s and 1970s, as the kibbutz economy expanded, and declined in the late 1980s, in response to campaigns by the federations and economic contraction (Russell 1996).

In negotiating new terms for their debt with the government in 1989 and 1990, the kibbutz federations committed their member kibbutzim to make more use of nonmember labor in the future, wherever this could

TABLE 2.3

Involvement of Nonmembers in Production and Services (Percentage of

	1990	1991	1992
Employment of Nonmembers			
Replacing members by outside labor	9.7	20.5	37.4
Increase in outside labor			
Hiring managers for businesses			12.5
Hiring office holders			
Nonmember as chair of board of business			
Nonmember as chair of board of community			
Joint Ventures and Partnerships			
Industrial partnerships with other kibbutzim	12.0	15.9	17.5
Partnerships with private investors	4.2	9.3	10.5
Agricultural cooperation with other kibbutzim			
Partner with other kibbutzim in services			
Partner with other kibbutzim in kindergarten			
Kibbutz industry in stock market			
Outsourcing services			
Hiring a contractor to run the kitchen			0.8
Buying meals from a contractor			
Selling Services to Outsiders			
Selling services to the outside	42.0	51.0	55.9
Accepting outsiders in educational system	30.9	52.7	68.0
Sale of houses to nonmembers			
Rental of housing to the outside			
Rental housing to kibbutz-born salaried employees			

help to increase the net income of the kibbutz. One way to overcome resistance to this among kibbutz members was to say that the use of hired labor was necessary to give individual members freedom to pursue specialized careers outside. Table 2.3 indicates that in 1990, only 9.7 percent of responding kibbutzim reported that they had adopted such a policy, but

Responding Kibbutzim Reporting Adoption of Innovations, by Year)

1993	1994	1995	1996	1997	1998	1999	2000	2001
40.5	49.3	43.7	46.5	44.5	41.5			
43.6	60.4	60.8	59.2	47.4	36.3			
16.4	26.1	28.2	34.2	51.0	56.5	59.8	50.0	47.6
			9.4	27.0	27.9	32.7	41.9	39.9
							38.0	51.3
						7.0		
17.5	16.8	20.5	21.8	20.7	21.0	18.9	22.3	22.9
11.0	12.1	14.5	19.3	24.9	31.1	32.6	35.5	33.9
				30.6	36.8	37.7	40.4	43.3
						5.1	3.2	4.5
							10.8	14.5
								4.7
1.2	2.9	4.2	5.1	6.4	9.5	10.3	13.2	20.0
							7.1	
56.6	58.7	63.9	58.9	65.5	67.8	62.0	68.9	72.2
68.8	76.9	80.7	89.7					
	1.6	0.8	0.8	1.6	5.0	4.7	8.1	7.0
		43.0	52.7	59.9	66.5	70.7	77.4	85.1
								65.6

in 1994 this proportion had grown to 49.3 percent. Whatever the reason, 43.6 percent of responding kibbutzim reported making it their policy to increase the use of outside labor in 1993, rising to 60.8 percent in 1995. Kibbutzim reporting that they were pursuing these policies declined in later years; often they would explain that the use of hired labor in their kibbutz was no longer changing, because it was already very high. Thus these two questions were dropped from the survey after 1998.

Although kibbutzim have been employing nonmembers for many decades, a new phenomenon of the 1990s was the hiring of nonmembers not only as laborers, but also as decision makers. In 1992, only 12.5 percent of kibbutzim reported hiring managers to run their businesses, but this proportion rose to half or more of all responding kibbutzim in the later years of the survey. In 1996, only 9.4 percent of kibbutzim reported that they were hiring nonmembers to hold kibbutz offices, but this rose to 41.9 percent in 2000. The percentage of kibbutzim reporting that they had a nonmember serving as the chair of the board of a business already stood at 40.7 percent when this issue entered the survey in 1999, and rose to 51.3 percent in 2001.

Turning such managerial functions over to outside specialists was a significant change for the kibbutzim. Degania had been established in opposition to the authority of the hired agronomist over agricultural workers at the training farm at Kinneret. Hiring professional managers was not just another instance of the employment of nonmembers. It also dealt a major blow to the ideal of self-governance, which had long been an important part of the ideology and self-image of the kibbutzim.

Besides employing nonmembers, many kibbutzim came into contact with nonmembers in other ways. One was participation by the kibbutz in joint ventures. Many of these joint ventures were in association with other kibbutzim. The percentage of kibbutzim participating in industrial partnerships with other kibbutzim rose from 12.0 percent in 1990 to 22.9 percent in 2001. In 2001, 43.3 percent of responding kibbutzim reported that they were involved in joint agricultural ventures with other kibbutzim, 14.5 percent were operating kindergartens in cooperation with other kibbutzim, and 4.5 percent were partnering in services with other kibbutzim.

Partnerships involving investors outside the kibbutz movement also became increasingly common during this period. The percentage of responding kibbutzim reporting that they were engaged in partnerships with private investors rose from 4.2 percent in 1990 to 35.5 percent in 2000, falling slightly to 33.9 percent in 2001. In 2001, 4.7 percent of responding kibbutzim reported that they had raised capital for their ventures by issuing publicly tradeable shares of stock.

Nonmembers also came to play increasing roles in the communal lives of many kibbutzim during this period. One way was through the outsourcing of services. The percentage of kibbutzim reporting that they had hired a contractor to run their kitchen rose from 0.8 percent in 1992 to 20.0 percent in 2001. In 2000, another 7.1 percent of kibbutzim reported that their kitchens were purchasing meals from an outside contractor.

Although this use of nonmembers as providers of services was occurring in only small numbers of kibbutzim, many more kibbutzim were welcoming nonmembers as recipients of services. The general policy of selling services to outsiders had been adopted by 42.0 percent of responding kibbutzim when the Institute's survey started in 1990, rising to 72.2 percent in 2001. The percentage of kibbutzim allowing children of nonmembers to participate in a given kibbutz's early childhood development system (ages 0 to 6) rose from 30.9 percent in 1990 to 89.7 percent in 1996.

Rental of kibbutz-owned housing to nonmembers had been adopted by 43.0 percent of kibbutzim when this question was first asked, in 1995, rising to 85.1 percent in 2001. At first, rental to outsiders was seen as a way to make productive use of housing that had been built for members and was currently vacant. Later, many kibbutzim built special neighborhoods for nonmembers; these new neighborhoods were viewed not as sources of rental income but as a way to revive communities that were both shrinking and aging, by providing children for the kindergartens, patients for the clinics, and patrons for other kibbutz services. The Israel Land Administration approved these projects, viewing them as a way to shift population from the crowded center to the less-developed periphery. In more recent years, the Israel Land Administration has asked the kibbutzim for 5 percent of the rental income earned from these projects, on the grounds that the land involved belongs not to the kibbutzim but to the nation.

In the later years of the survey, some kibbutzim began not only to rent but to sell houses to nonmembers. The proportion of kibbutzim reporting that they had taken this step rose from 1 percent to 2 percent per year, from 1994 through 1997, to 5 percent in 1998 and 1999 and 7 percent to 8 percent in 2000 and 2001.

Whereas kibbutz members had once lived and worked almost entirely with other kibbutz members, they now came into contact with nonmembers as co-workers, as customers, and as neighbors. When two people encountered one another on a kibbutz in these years, it was increasingly likely that at least one of them was a nonmember (Getz 1998b). The transformation of the kibbutzim from communities of intimate acquaintances into associations characterized by relations among strangers, of which Erik Cohen (1983) had already noted early signs in the 1970s, was now even farther along. Insofar as the unique practices of the kibbutzim had previously gained stability from the isolation of the community from contact with the world outside (Kanter 1968), these walls were beginning to come down.

Changes in Relations between Kibbutzim and Members

The most numerous changes being considered and adopted by the kibbutzim during the 1990s dealt neither with kibbutz management nor with the role of outsiders, but directly altered the relationship between the kibbutzim and individual members. These changes fell into three general categories: new rights and entitlements for kibbutz members; privatization of consumption and services; and changes in compensation and ownership. In all three of these categories, kibbutz members acquired new freedoms and claims on kibbutz assets at the expense of the communal household and economy.

Rights of Members and Children

Of the reforms spreading among kibbutzim during this period, one set aimed to increase the rights and financial security of individuals within the kibbutz. The crisis that beset the kibbutzim in the late 1980s was demographic as well as economic. In those years, members and their adult children left the kibbutzim in large numbers. Subsequently, the kibbutzim introduced a wide range of reforms aimed at making the kibbutz more attractive to current and future members by offering new rights and entitlements to members and their adult children.

In a traditional kibbutz, members participated in the various forms of productive and service activities, as directed by the kibbutz; members and their children who wished to pursue careers in specialized occupations not required on the kibbutz had no alternative but to leave. As the kibbutzim negotiated new terms for their debt with the government in the late 1980s, economists inside and outside the government recommended that, if a kibbutz member could earn more money for the kibbutz by working outside the kibbutz economy, that member should be permitted to take the outside job. The kibbutz federations agreed to this reform because it promised to increase not only the incomes of kibbutzim, but also the opportunities open to individual members.

Table 2.4 indicates that, in 1990, the first year of the Institute's survey, 34.9 percent of responding kibbutzim reported that they permitted members to work outside. In 2001, the last year of the survey, this percentage had risen to 73.5 percent. A related reform was the growing acceptance of the principle that it was the responsibility of the individual member, not of the kibbutz, to identify the most appropriate use of that member's skills. In 1990, only 7.8 percent of responding kibbutzim reported that they had adopted this principle; in 2001, the figure had increased to 69.0 percent.

In 1992, 9,700 adults living on kibbutzim commuted to outside jobs. This constituted 12.5 percent of the kibbutz labor force. By 2001, this number had nearly doubled, to 18,500 (27.1 percent of the kibbutz labor force in that year) (Pavin 2007, 9). Kibbutz members who took outside jobs found their professional and career opportunities greatly expanded, but their relationship to the kibbutz was simultaneously dramatically altered. For kibbutz members who commuted to jobs in nearby cities, the kibbutz took on the character of a gated bedroom community. Such members became less and less involved in the day-to-day problems of the kibbutz, and, for long periods of time, might not even see other kibbutz members.

As kibbutz members pursued more diverse lifestyles on and off the kibbutz, it became increasingly unrealistic to expect all of them to be able to attend and participate in meetings of the General Assembly. New polling methods adopted by many kibbutzim enabled members to cast votes without being at meetings or even identifying themselves. Advocates of voting by secret ballot claimed that this would preserve and strengthen the direct democracy of the kibbutz, by making it possible for more members to vote. Opponents objected that the secret ballot would reduce the deliberative aspect of kibbutz decision making, making it harder to achieve

TABLE 2.4

New Rights and Entitlements for Members and Kibbutz-Born Adults

(Percentage of Responding Kibbutzim Reporting Adoption of Innovations, by Year)

	1990	1991	1992	1993	1994	1995	1996	1997	1998	1999	2000	2001
Secret ballot	3.8	11.3	26.4	33.6	35.3	43.0	48.1	48.3	57.3	55.2	61.5	67.8
Members working outside the kibbutz	34.9	46.7	64.6	54.8	58.7	60.1	58.1	63.1	71.3	73.5		
Member responsibility in selection of work	7.8	12.3	25.5	27.3	35.2	35.9	41.6	44.1	54.5	59.2	68.8	69.0
Pension plan		22.1	35.6	43.4	52.9	65.0	71.2	72.4	67.8	73.4	81.8	84.7
Health insurance											63.6	71.0
Payment of higher education expenses of kibbutz-born											36.6	44.4
Rental of housing to kibbutz-born young adults											53.8	65.2
Cash grants to kibbutz-born young adults											31.1	35.6

consensus or even to explicate differing points of view. In 1990, only 3.8 percent of responding kibbutzim allowed members to vote by secret ballot; in 2001, the proportion using the secret ballot had risen to 67.8 percent.

In a traditional kibbutz, the kibbutz pays the medical expenses of its members, and continues to provide for members when they can no longer work. Retired members live in kibbutz housing, eat in the kibbutz dining hall, and pay other expenses out of a modest monthly stipend provided by the kibbutz. Members saw no need for a pension, because they considered the kibbutz as their pension, which they expected to take care of them for the rest of their lives.

After Kibbutz Beit Oren collapsed, both economically and socially, in 1986, many kibbutz members began to wonder where they would live and who would take care of them should their own kibbutz fail. Members could no longer simply trust that their kibbutz would be able to support them no matter what. To insure members against this new risk, collapse, many kibbutzim began to make annual contributions toward individual pensions for each member. When this issue first appeared on the Institute's survey, in 1991, 22.1 percent of kibbutzim had established pension plans for members; by 2001, that proportion had climbed to 84.7 percent. For similar reasons, most kibbutzim (71 percent in 2001) began purchasing health insurance for their members.

In Israel, all young men and women serve in the armed forces for two to four years after leaving high school. When they complete military service, many spend several months to one or two years traveling in other countries before beginning their college educations. This means that Israeli young adults often spend ten or more years in a prolonged state of adolescence, during which they keep returning to their parents' homes between periods spent in military service, in traveling abroad, and in educational institutions.

Outside the kibbutzim, what Israeli families do and do not owe their adult children is negotiated one household at a time. Within a kibbutz, it requires the formulation of explicit communal policies. In the past, kibbutzim permitted kibbutz-born young adults to stay at the kibbutz free of charge during a "moratorium" period; when such young adults stayed at the kibbutz, they received a budget from the kibbutz and were expected to work just as if they were members. When abroad or studying, they could keep the apartment involved.

In the 1990s, kibbutzim began to allow kibbutz-born adults to live for indefinite periods as tenants in kibbutz-owned housing, in return for monthly payments of rent. By the year 2000, when this series of questions was first added to the survey, 53.8 percent of responding kibbutzim reported that they permitted kibbutz-born young adults to rent subsidized apartments from the kibbutz. In 2001, this figure had risen to 65.2 percent. In that year, 9,792 kibbutz-born adults were living on kibbutzim as nonmembers; they constituted 13 percent of the total adult population of the kibbutzim (Arbel 2004).

In addition to allowing kibbutz-born young adults to live on the kibbutz in subsidized housing, many kibbutzim helped them in other ways. Kibbutzim giving cash grants to kibbutz-born young adults came to 31.1 percent of responding kibbutzim in 2000, 35.6 percent in 2001. Many kibbutzim also took steps to enhance educational opportunities for the children of members. The kibbutzim had historically paid all higher educational expenses of members and their children, but opportunities to go to college were rationed according to seniority, and kibbutz-born young adults found themselves at the bottom of these waiting lists. In the 1990s, many kibbutzim established new programs to pay the higher education expenses of kibbutz-born young adults, provided that they work in the kibbutz at least one year before going to college, and an additional 90 to 120 days following their graduation for each year of education. The percentage of kibbutzim that had introduced such arrangements was 36.6 percent in 2000, 44.4 percent in 2001.

Privatizing Consumption and Services

In a traditional kibbutz, income is earned collectively and is also spent collectively. Members eat in the communal dining hall, sleep in kibbutz-owned housing, and take a dip after work in a kibbutz-owned swimming pool. Trips abroad are rationed, but when a member's turn comes, the travel expenses are paid by the kibbutz. Until the 1980s, even childrearing on most kibbutzim was collective, with children sleeping in children's houses.

Although public perceptions of the kibbutz continued to emphasize these collective elements, consumption patterns on Israeli kibbutzim had in practice been becoming less collective and more individual for many years (Ben-Ner 1987). Parents sought opportunities to spend more time with their children, and the kibbutzim built apartments large enough to accommodate both parents and children. By the late 1980s, many kibbutz members were eating their morning and evening meals in their apartments, and came to the kibbutz dining hall only for lunch.

As the locus of consumption has shifted to individuals and households, many kibbutzim have transferred responsibility for making many kinds of consumption decisions from the collective to the household. One of the earliest forms this took was the adoption of a so-called comprehensive budget, in which the allocation paid by the kibbutz to each household was augmented to cover certain consumption expenditures that were previously paid for by the kibbutz. In 1990, when the Institute's survey began, 31.6 percent of responding kibbutzim reported that they had adopted comprehensive budgeting. In 1996, this proportion had risen to 74.7 percent, as shown in table 2.5.

One of the first consumption expenses to be transferred from the community to individual households was the cost of electricity. Summers in Israel can be very hot, tempting kibbutz members and their children to make heavy use of the air conditioners in their apartments. On a traditional kibbutz, the cost of electricity was paid by the kibbutz. If one kibbutz household used energy more wastefully than another, that family paid no financial penalty. The kibbutz had no way even to find out which households used more or less electricity, because individual apartments did not have meters. In the 1990s, most Israeli kibbutzim installed meters to monitor electricity use by each household, and began requiring members to pay for the electricity each used. In 1990, only 8.2 percent of responding kibbutzim reported that they had introduced this reform, but by 2001 this figure had risen to 79.6 percent.

As responsibility for increasing numbers of consumption expenses was shifted from the kibbutz as a whole to individual households, it became common among kibbutz members to refer to such reforms as instances of privatization (e.g., Getz 1994). Amir Helman noted at the time that this was a "strange use of the fashionable concept of privatization" (1994, 23). Whereas in the Great Britain of Margaret Thatcher and the transitional economies of Eastern Europe, *privatization* referred to the sale of state-owned enterprises to private owners, among the kibbutzim of the 1990s, the term was being applied to "any decision to decrease the collective's expenditure in order to increase the personal budget" (Helman 1994, 23). Helman pointed to the way kibbutz members spoke about the new arrangements to pay for electricity as an instance of this word usage:

TABLE 2.5.

Privatization of Services (Percentage of Responding

	1990	1991	1992
Privatization of Education and Childrearing			
Having parents' budget include enrichment	3.8	4.2	8.5
Including higher education in members' budgets	0.4	0.8	2.4
Having special expenses for kids in parents' budgets	0.8	0.0	0.8
Young to study by special agreement			
Privatization of education			
Privatization of Consumption			
Comprehensive budget	31.6	44.2	54.9
Pay for electricity	8.2	20.4	37.6
Pay for meals	0.0	1.1	2.4
Pay for recreation	13.5	20.5	26.2
Pay for travel		24.6	38.7
Okay to own or use private car			8.9
Okay to increase size of house at own expense			
Privatization of health services			
Privatization of the laundry			
Closing or Cutting Back Services			
Canceling breakfast in dining hall		6.5	7.9
Canceling evening meal in dining hall		8.4	11.9
Closing of services		2.8	5.3
Closing of dining hall			

"For example, if the General Assembly decided that each family should pay for its own consumption of electricity (instead of the typical kibbutz total payment for all of its members), then the members would say that they had 'privatized' the electricity budget" (1994, 23).

By 2001, most responding kibbutzim reported that they had also privatized expenditures for recreation (58.1 percent) and for travel (86.4 percent).

Kibbutzim Reporting Adoption of Innovations, by Year)

1993	1994	1995	1996	1997	1998	1999	2000	2001
9.0	13.2	13.4	12.6	17.8	23.0	25.4	29.1	34.8
4.1	4.9	5.5	8.1	8.0	9.2	14.5	17.9	22.9
0.8	1.7	3.2	3.4					
73.0	78.4	76.8	73.1	76.9	79.4	79.0		
				2.9	8.4	8.3	16.5	22.8
59.0	59.9	68.7	74.7					
41.6	52.4	58.8	64.0	66.8	72.4	75.5	78.4	79.6
5.4	11.3	17.3	30.5	41.9	58.3	65.8	68.2	70.6
28.6	30.2	31.0	37.0	40.8	47.2	52.4	59.0	58.1
44.1	51.5	56.6	67.4	70.0	78.2	82.2	79.6	86.4
11.7	18.8	29.8	37.2	46.1	52.0	60.5	64.0	67.8
	11.7	14.0	17.3	21.4	34.3	37.2	45.9	48.8
			2.5	4.2	8.4	8.3	19.1	26.1
					18.3	24.2	30.4	38.1
8.8	12.1	13.0	17.2	21.0	28.6	35.7	37.7	47.0
14.5	22.2	27.8	38.0	48.7	59.0	66.7	65.5	68.5
4.1	3.8	4.5	4.2	5.4	6.8	9.2	11.0	13.0
						6.6	8.9	9.1

In 70.6 percent of responding kibbutzim, members were now being charged for the meals they ate in the communal dining hall. In 67.8 percent, members were free to own or use private cars. Large and growing minorities of kibbutzim also had voted to privatize their health services (26.1 percent) or laundry (38.1 percent), and about half (48.8 percent) were letting members increase the size of their homes at their own expense.

In light of the widespread use of the term *privatization* to refer to many such changes then taking place on the kibbutzim, Helman suggested in 1994 that one "may prefer a broader definition of privatization" that has the scope to cover these. Helman recommended thinking of privatization not as "the simple formal transferal of ownership," but as "a system which transfers power from the center to the individual." By "using this broad definition for privatization," Helman concluded, "it is possible to show that the kibbutz is now in the middle of a strong privatization process" (1994, 24).

Proposals to privatize expenditures on education and children were slower to spread than proposals to privatize other consumption expenses. "Privatization of education" had been endorsed by 2.9 percent of kibbutzim in 1997, rising to 22.8 percent in 2001. Paying costs of higher education out of members' budgets had been adopted by 0.4 percent in 1990, growing to 22.9 percent in 2001. Including enrichment expenses for children in their parents' budgets spread from 3.8 percent of responding kibbutzim in 1990 to 34.8 percent in 2001. The most popular reform in this group was a policy of allowing young persons to study by special agreement, in use in 73 percent to 79 percent of responding kibbutzim between 1993 and 1999.

Although some kibbutz-provided services had now to be paid for, others were being cut back or closed. In 2001, 68.5 percent of responding kibbutzim said that they had cancelled the evening meal in their dining hall, and 47.0 percent had cancelled breakfast; in 9.1 percent, the dining hall had been entirely closed. The percentage of kibbutzim reporting that they had adopted "closing of services" as a policy rose from 2.8 percent in 1991 to 13.0 percent in 2001.

Rewards and Incentives

In a traditional kibbutz, the production and distribution of income follow the principle of "from each according to his or her ability, to each according to his or her need." By earning incomes and owning assets collectively rather than individually, the classic kibbutzim sought to appeal to the socialist and Zionist ideals of their founders. Even if the members of a traditional kibbutz had wanted to make greater use of material incentives, they would not have found this easy. When housing, meals, and recreation are provided free of charge, what would a member need money for? As expenditures of kibbutz households have been privatized, however, the uses and need for additional income in these households have grown. This in turn has opened kibbutzim to the possibility of using material incentives to motivate and reward members' work.

The earliest proposals for the use of material incentives on kibbutzim continued to assign all kibbutz members a budget on the basis of need, but made it possible for members to earn additions to these budgeted amounts by working extra hours or days. Paying members for overtime or additional work was reported by only one kibbutz in 1990, but the proportion using this form of payment had risen to 35.8 percent of responding kibbutzim in 2001, as shown in table 2.6. Paying members for working an extra day on the Sabbath was reported by 25.2 percent of kibbutzim in 1999, rising to 43.4 percent in 2001. Paying for additional work in services rose from 17.5 percent to 33.0 percent during these same years, and payment for seasonal work in so-called gius rose to 31.8 percent.

Despite the growing popularity of these specific forms of additional payment, the kibbutzim were slow to declare a general policy of connecting days worked and a member's budget. Such a policy was reported by 2.8 percent of kibbutzim in 1992, rising to 18.1 percent in 1999. In 2000 and 2001, the Institute divided this question into two parts, asking separately whether the kibbutz paid its members additional pay for additional days worked, and whether it reduced members' pay for reduced days worked. In both years, reduced pay for reduced days worked was the more widespread of the two policies: 14 percent or 12 percent versus 7 percent.

Although the opportunity to earn extra pay by working extra days was open to all kibbutz members, other proposed rewards and incentives were targeted at certain categories of jobs or members. Pay for officeholders in difficult jobs was reported by just one kibbutz in 1990, rising to 3.5 percent in 1996. Paying additions to members' budgets on a basis of seniority was reported by 10.0 percent of kibbutzim in 1996, rising to 31.1 percent in 2001.

Two innovations under consideration during this period went beyond these piecemeal amendments to traditional kibbutz budgets, and instead replaced them with new systems of compensation.

The less radical of these was known as an integrated budget. Usually such budgets had three components: (1) the major component, based on the previous monetary budget; (2) a differential monetary allocation based on the member's seniority; and (3) a differential allocation based on the market

TABLE 2.6.

Material Rewards and Incentives (Percentage of Responding

	1990	1991	1992
Extra Pay for Extra Work			
Pay for overtime or additional work	0.4	2.0	4.8
Pay for officeholders in difficult jobs	0.4	0.8	1.6
Connection between days worked and budget			2.8
Additional amount budgeted for seniority			
Payment for work on the Sabbath			
Payment for additional work in services			
Payment for seasonal work in "gius"			
Additional pay for additional days worked			
Reduced pay for reduced days worked			
Differential Salaries			
Budget with differential salary component			
Payment of differential salary			
Transfer of ownership to individual members			
Distribution of kibbutz shares			
Transfer of kibbutz assets			
Limited transfer of kibbutz assets			
Transfer of ownership of all assets to members			
Inheritance of rights			

salary of the member's occupation. There are differences among kibbutzim in the proportion of total pay represented by this third differential salary component, ranging from 3 percent to 30 percent, most commonly near 20 percent.

The more radical new form of compensation was the so-called safety-net budget, which began to be used in such kibbutzim as Gesher Haziv and Naot Mordechai in 1995. Under this system, members were paid differential salaries, based entirely on the market value of their labor. Whether members worked inside or outside the kibbutz, they usually would have to pay two types of taxes to the community, one that was the same for all payers, and another

Kibbutzim Reporting Adoption of Innovations, by Year)

1993	1994	1995	1996	1997	1998	1999	2000	2001
2.8	5.4	8.9	10.9	17.9	25.2	24.4	29.4	35.8
0.0	2.6	2.3	3.5					
2.1	4.2	6.1	8.4	10.8	16.8	18.1		
			10.0	14.9	19.8	25.3	29.8	31.1
						25.2	37.5	43.4
						17.5	28.6	33.0
						21.9	29.8	31.8
							7.1	7.1
							13.8	11.6
			2.9	6.3	7.6	11.2	14.3	15.0
	0.8	0.0	0.8	3.8	5.9	7.0	14.7	23.6
	0.0	0.0	0.0	0.0	0.4	0.9	6.2	
			0.0	0.8	0.8	0.0	0.0	1.0
						4.6	5.8	3.1
							8.7	2.5
						1.5		

based on income. The fixed tax would cover municipal expenses, such as land-scaping, refuse collection, and road maintenance. The tax based on income served as one of the sources for a safety net to meet the needs of the weaker population, such as elderly or sick members. This budgetary system is often referred to as either a safety-net budget or a full-differential salary.

Payment of differential salaries spread slowly in the 1990s. It was reported by just one kibbutz in 1994 and in 1996, 3.8 percent in 1997, 5.9 percent in 1998, and 7.0 percent in 1999. During these years, more kibbutzim used mixed-compensation systems, combining budgets with salaries, than paid differential salaries alone. Mixed-compensation systems were reported by 2.9 percent of responding kibbutzim in 1996, 11.2 percent in 1999, and 15.0 percent in 2001. In 2000, payment of differential salaries for the first time became more widespread than the mixed-compensation systems, being reported by 14.7 percent of responding kibbutzim in 2000 and by 23.6 percent in 2001.

Finally, there were reforms that transferred ownership of some or all kibbutz assets from the kibbutz as a whole to individual members. Table 2.6 shows their incidence. These innovations were the slowest to spread during this period. Distribution of kibbutz shares to members was reported by no kibbutzim in 1994–1997, one kibbutz in 1998, two kibbutzim in 1999, and 6.2 percent in 2000. "Transfer of kibbutz assets" was never reported by more than two kibbutzim in any year, but the proportion reporting "limited transfer of kibbutz assets" rose to 5.8 percent in 2001.

From Reform to Transformation

Taken together, tables 2.2–2.6 document the gradual diffusion of numerous modest reforms during this period, coupled with a general reluctance to make major changes. The division of labor on kibbutzim became increasingly complex, but most kibbutzim refused to abolish the principle of rotating managers. Many kibbutz members now worked outside the kibbutz, but the income earned from that outside employment continued to be paid to the kibbutz, not the individual member. A growing portion of consumption expenditures had become private rather than public, but most members' budgets continued to be based not on work but on need.

The five tables show that the most widely adopted reforms were those that expanded the role of nonmembers, increased the rights and entitlements of members, and privatized consumption. By 2001, most kibbutzim had decided, at some time or other, to increase the use of outside labor, and were ready to hire outside managers to run one or more of their businesses. Most were partnering with other kibbutzim in agricultural ventures, selling services to outsiders, and welcoming outsiders in their schools and rental apartments. New rights and entitlements gaining general acceptance included secret ballots, pension plans, health insurance, members' working outside the kibbutz, and rental of housing to the kibbutz-born. In consumption, most kibbutzim had adopted comprehensive budgeting, required members to pay for their own electricity, meals, and travel, and were permitting members to own or use private cars. Most had also cancelled the evening meals in their dining halls on all evenings except Fridays.

In the later years of the survey, a growing minority of kibbutzim was going beyond these widespread, relatively modest changes, and was beginning to introduce differential systems of payment. In 2001, 15.0 percent of responding kibbutzim reported using mixed systems of compensation, and another 23.6 percent reported having introduced full-differential payment.

Reforms that remained least successful in this period were clustered in two groups: changes in decision making, and changes in ownership or compensation. Of the changes in decision making, only three were widely adopted: boards of directors for industrial ventures, human resource divisions, and differential shadow wages. Reforms adopted among only a minority of kibbutzim were: representative councils, additional uses for boards of directors, incorporation of branches, and internal control committees.

This pattern of mixed and partial success for changes involving decision making, coupled with more widespread adoption of other changes, is consistent with findings reported by Menachem Topel (2005). According to Topel, proposals to change the economic structure of a kibbutz and its methods of decision making are initiated by "the technocrats," while aspirations for privatization and expansion of individual freedom tend to come from "the non-technocrats"; these two agendas converge to produce a "coalition of interests" that votes in favor of change but lacks shared aspirations.

Conclusions

Comparing this description of reforms introduced by the kibbutzim in the 1990s to the summary, in chapter 1, of trends affecting the kibbutzim in the 1970s and 1980s, it is clear that the changes of the 1990s are continuous in many ways with those of the previous decades. Both the kibbutz economy and the kibbutz community continued to become more differentiated and more individuated. The use of hired labor and other forms of contact between members and nonmembers continued to grow in prevalence. Family-centered housing had become the norm before 1990, and the so-called comprehensive budget that effectively privatized household budgets had already been introduced on 31.6 percent of kibbutzim by 1990, when the surveys of the Institute for Research of the Kibbutz began. The most innovative reforms widely adopted in the 1990s were the pensions and health insurance, both of which were aimed to make sure that the kibbutzim would continue to meet the needs of elderly members in the future as they had in the past. Although the solutions were new, the problems created by the aging of the kibbutz membership had already begun to receive increasing recognition and attention in the previous decade.

Although the changes most widely adopted in the 1990s were those that were most compatible with legal definitions and recent trends, a minority of kibbutzim was beginning to make more radical changes. The introduction of safety-net budgets required the affected kibbutzim to amend their bylaws, and forced the kibbutz movement and the Israeli government to consider whether kibbutzim that paid differential salaries were still entitled to call themselves kibbutzim.

Although only small numbers of kibbutzim began paying differential salaries to members in the 1990s, most kibbutzim introduced reforms during this period that would contribute, in numerous ways, to this later change. Most kibbutzim kept open their collective dining halls, but members now had to pay for meals there; after all, until expenses for food, recreation, and travel had been privatized, kibbutz members who earned high salaries would have had nothing on which to spend their higher incomes.

More generally, the reforms of the 1990s contributed to the later and larger changes by serving as a period in which the kibbutzim lost "organizational inertia." During these years, the process of change in the kibbutzim had been institutionalized (Rosner and Cohen 1994) at every level of Israeli society. The state in its role as creditor had demanded reforms, and the kibbutz federations had agreed to these. Change committees had been established on every kibbutz, and virtually every kibbutz had adopted at least some of the reforms listed in tables 2.2–2.6.

We take up the story of how individual kibbutzim made the decision to adopt safety-net budgets in chapter 4, and of how the movement and government responded to this change in chapter 5. In chapter 3 we address questions not yet answered regarding the spread of reforms among kibbutzim in the 1990s. Whereas in chapter 2 we have focused on which reforms were adopted and which were not, in chapter 3 we look more closely at the processes through which changes were adopted, and at differences among kibbutzim in their attitudes toward change.

3

Consideration and Adoption of Innovations, 1990–2001

In chapter 2 we documented the spread of innovations through the population of kibbutzim. Although some innovations enjoyed wide acceptance, others were introduced in only small numbers of kibbutzim. In this chapter, we shift from the question of which changes were accepted, to the question of how individual kibbutzim made and carried out decisions to adopt them.

We first demonstrate that kibbutzim did not make these decisions quickly or easily. Most proposed reforms went through lengthy periods of discussion and preparation before they were put into use. Many decisions were hotly contested, and kibbutzim often changed their plans for innovations after having accepted them.

Later in this chapter, we examine differences among kibbutzim in their readiness to adopt innovations. We estimate the effects of variables identified in previous studies as potentially important influences on the likelihood that democratic and communal organizations would abandon their unique practices. These variables include the size, age, and economic condition of organizations, their ideology, and whether they are geographically isolated. Because kibbutzim share with other organizations both a capacity for what Michael Hannan and John Freeman term organizational inertia (1984) and a tendency to imitate the behavior of other organizations of their type (Ahmadjian and Robinson 2001; DiMaggio and Powell 1983), our analyses also take into account the effects of these influences.

In the University of Haifa's annual surveys of changes among kibbutzim (Getz 1994, 1998a), informants were asked which of six responses best characterized the relationship between their kibbutz and each change: "We are not considering'" it, "We have rejected" it, "We are discussing" it, "We have decided" to use it, "We are implementing" it, or "We are using" it. In this chapter, we begin by examining the distribution of responses across all six of these categories. Whereas in chapter 2 we looked only at which percentage of kibbutzim reported that they were currently "using" an innovation, we in this chapter give equal attention to reports that a kibbutz is "discussing" an innovation, has "rejected" it, has "decided" in favor of an innovation but not yet acted, or is currently in the process of "implementing" it.

After examining the frequencies with which kibbutzim reported that they had rejected, were discussing, or were in the process of implementing innovations, we ask how responses in one year are related to those in the next. For example, do kibbutzim that, in one year, give the response that a given change had been rejected give the same response in the next year? Or is rejection often followed by further discussion, which in turn may lead to adoption of the innovation in a later year? What about the response that a change is under discussion? Does "We are discussing it" mean that the organization has embarked on a series of steps leading to eventual use of the innovation, or does it reflect a level of commitment to the innovation that remains low? Similarly, do periods of having "decided" in favor of, or being in the process of "implementing," an innovation reflect merely technical and temporary delays, or do these responses signify unexpected obstacles and second thoughts?

Only after addressing these preliminary issues do we, in this chapter, present the third and final stage of this analysis, asking: Which influences lead a kibbutz to change its answer regarding a given reform from one year to another? Which characteristics of organizations and of changes increase the likelihood of movements toward use of innovations, and which promote movements away? And do the answers to these questions differ from one stage of the process of considering and introducing innovations to another?

Processes of Deliberation and Implementation

As noted, in later portions of this chapter we give increasing attention to how responses by kibbutzim in one year are related to responses they give in the next. To make these analyses possible, it was necessary to create a data set that consisted of pairs of observations of the same innovation in the same kibbutz in two consecutive years; this produced a total of 36,592 pairs of observations. Before addressing the issue of how responses from one year compared to those from the next, we examine the distribution of responses for these pairs in the first year.

The distribution of responses among the six possible answers is shown in table 3.1. For most innovations, the most common response in most years of the survey was that the kibbutz was "not considering" that innovation; a total of 20,964, or 56.7 percent of all paired observations, begin with this response. The second most common response was that a kibbutz was currently "using" the innovation in question; another 8,732 pairs, or 23.6 percent, begin with this response.

In nearly a fifth of all cases (19.7 percent), remarkably, the stance of a kibbutz toward a given innovation in the initial year was neither that the kibbutz was not considering the innovation, nor that it was currently using it, but something in between. We begin by taking a close look at the

TABLE 3.1.

Frequencies of Responses to Questions about Innovations

Response	No. of responses	As % of responses
Not considering	20,964	56.7
Rejected	372	1.0
Discussing	4,907	13.3
Decided to adopt	928	2.5
Implementing	1,061	2.9
Using	8,732	23.6
Total	36,964	100.0

innovations most likely to evoke each of these four intermediate responses. Insofar as any of these intermediate responses are stages that most or all organizations go through as they make orderly transitions from "not considering" an innovation to currently "using" it, then the innovations that most frequently attract these four intermediate responses should be the innovations most widely adopted during the period of the survey, as shown in tables 2.2–2.6. If, on the other hand, innovations attract these responses only to the extent that they raise special problems, then the innovations most frequently listed as "rejected," "under discussion," "decided," or "in implementation" will not be the widely adopted innovations.

The innovations most frequently reported as having been rejected or under discussion are not those most popular, but those most controversial. The two most frequently rejected innovations are proposals to privatize health services (5.1 percent of responses) or to privatize education (4.4 percent). Other frequently rejected proposals would pay differential salaries (3.1 percent), pay extra for overtime or additional work (2.5 percent), or introduce budgets that would include a differential salary component.

Innovations most frequently reported as being under discussion are, again, largely a set of controversial proposals for new forms of compensation. These include proposals to make additional increments to budgets on the basis of seniority (35.5 percent), to create a connection between days worked and budgets (28.2 percent), or to introduce budgets with differential salary components (24.4 percent). Other changes that arouse high frequencies of discussion include creation of an internal control committee (26.2 percent) and proposals to transfer kibbutz assets to individual members (25.8 percent).

Innovations most frequently reported as decided for, or in process of implementation, in contrast, include many of the innovations identified in tables 2.2–2.6 as having been adopted by most kibbutzim. Since these two responses can be given only after innovations have been approved, it is not surprising that they arise primarily about innovations that are being widely introduced.

Pension plans are more likely than any other changes to be reported as decided but not yet implemented. An average of 6.6 percent of kibbutzim gave this response for this innovation, during the years of the survey; another 6.9 percent of kibbutzim indicated that they were in the process of implementing this innovation. Charging members for electricity is the next most likely to be reported as decided, at 5.9 percent of responses, and also ranks high among innovations most likely to be reported as in the process of implementation, with 8.8 percent. Other innovations that attract high frequencies of both responses are proposals to create partnerships with private investors (5.8 percent decided, 4.4 percent implementing), and establishing boards of directors for industrial ventures (4.2 percent decided, 4.2 percent implementing).

Some widespread changes are adopted without going through periods of being listed as having been decided or in process of implementation. Voting by secret ballot, allowing members to work outside the kibbutz, renting housing to nonmembers, and canceling the evening meal are among a number of popular changes that rarely fall into these intermediate statuses.

It is not difficult to infer reasons why some changes might be more likely than others to encounter delays after members have approved them. The decision to charge members for electricity cannot be put into practice until meters have been installed in each household. Pension plans require detailed designs and mechanisms for funding. Rights that do not create financial obligations, such as voting by secret ballot and allowing members to work outside, can more readily be implemented without delay. Creating boards of directors for industrial ventures requires both establishing new legal structures and identifying and recruiting individuals to fill the new roles, and therefore takes time. Canceling evening meals merely shortens the number of hours during which the dining hall is in operation, and can therefore be introduced quickly.

Comparing the four intermediate responses on the basis of the innovations that most frequently evoke them, they appear to represent two distinctly different ways by which innovations can be stopped or delayed, on the path from not being considered to currently being used. Reports that an innovation is under discussion, like reports of rejection, signify that an innovation is controversial and has encountered opposition. Delays between acceptance and actual use of innovations, on the other hand, may be caused by technical and financial requirements of innovations, rather than signifying any reluctance to carry them out.

In table A.1 of the appendix, we shed additional light on the meaning of these intermediate responses by comparing the response given by a kibbutz, to each question in each year, to the response given by the same kibbutz to the same question in the following year. These analyses make two points that add to the significance of the intermediate responses. First, few kibbutzim pass directly from not considering an innovation in one year to using that innovation in the next; most innovations first pass through periods of discussion or implementation before being put into use. Second, although the likelihood of eventual adoption of an innovation increases as responses move from "discussing" to "decided" to "implementing," the risk that an innovation will be abandoned remains substantial at every stage.

Influences on Changes in Responses

In the remainder of this chapter, we identify factors that influence year-to-year transitions among the responses shown in table 3.1. We describe the potential influences on these changes in responses from year to year. Details regarding measurement are deferred to the appendix; the aim here is simply to identify potential influences and why they are included.

Economic Condition

All accounts of the reforms that have swept the kibbutzim over the past two decades begin with the economic crisis of the late 1980s. Individually and collectively, the kibbutzim fell into bankruptcy. Kibbutz Beit Oren collapsed both economically and socially in 1988, leading kibbutz members all over Israel to wonder how they would support themselves in the future if their own kibbutz were to fail. The Likud government and Israeli banks insisted that the kibbutzim promise to reform their structures as a condition of coming out of bankruptcy. Most kibbutzim, and the two major federations, made these pledges willingly, because these economic shocks were leading their own members to call for reforms.

Although this account comes to us anecdotally, it is also what we would expect on the basis of theory. According to Christine Oliver's (1992) theory of deinstitutionalization, organizations are most likely to abandon institutionalized practices when scarcities of resources make it increasingly difficult to afford the costs of continuing them. On the basis of this theory, we would expect to find that kibbutzim most affected by the economic crisis would be most likely to introduce these changes.

Further support for this expectation comes from the research of Tal Simons and Paul Ingram (1997) into the use of hired labor among Israeli kibbutzim in the years 1951 to 1965, and from later studies of the kibbutzim. Building on the earlier work of Haim Barkai (1977), Simons and Ingram viewed the avoidance of hired labor as an ideologically driven practice that reduces the income of kibbutzim adhering to it. These authors predicted and found that the more dependent kibbutzim were on loans from banks, the more likely they were to use hired labor. Studies of the adoption of changes by kibbutzim since 1990 have also often reported an inverse relationship between the economic condition of a kibbutz and its readiness to introduce reforms (e.g., Abramitzsky 2008; Ben-Rafael 1997; Russell, Hanneman, and Getz 2006).

Although much empirical evidence and theoretical argument lead us to expect a negative relationship between the economic condition of a kibbutz and the likelihood that it will introduce innovations, an alternative theoretical tradition predicts a positive relationship between economic condition and change. In the literature on democratic workplaces, the perceived degeneration of cooperative practices is often seen as a consequence of not hardship but prosperity. Democratic firms of many kinds have been accused of becoming more likely to abandon democratic structures, the more capital they accumulate or the more profitable they become (e.g., Ben-Ner 1984, 1988; Russell and Hanneman 1995). In a history of utopian communities in the United States, similarly, Rosabeth Kanter (1968) identifies sacrifice and ascetic renunciation of worldly pleasures as characteristics that help to make some of these organizations unusually long-lived. The implication of this literature is that, the more affluent they become, the more communal organizations like kibbutzim become tempted to introduce changes.

To measure the economic condition of individual kibbutzim, we use an index of economic crisis developed by kibbutz movement economists. This measure combines data on debt, profit, liquidity, and living expenses to produce a composite score for each kibbutz. Scores range from 0 to 100, with 0 to 30 signifying that the condition of the kibbutz is "good," 31 to 50 indicating that it is "OK," 51 to 65 that it "needs improvement," 66 to 80 that it shows "hidden crisis," and 81 to 100 that it shows "active crisis" (Yoffe 2005, 47).

Change in Number of Members

The problems that shook the kibbutzim in the late 1980s were not only economic, but also demographic. As they lost faith in the economic future of their kibbutzim, many kibbutz members and adult children of members left to pursue more attractive opportunities elsewhere. Some authors (e.g., Rosenblatt and Sheaffer 2001; Sheaffer and Helman 1994) have asserted that the kibbutzim had become subject to a process of negative selection, or "brain drain," in which the most productive members depart and the least productive remain. Since the late 1980s, calls for reform of the kibbutzim have aimed not only to make the kibbutzim more efficient and productive, but also to make them more attractive to present and future members.

Once more, this anecdotal evidence is consistent with the expectations that can be derived from relevant organizational theories, such as that of Oliver (1992). From this perspective, the loss of members can be viewed as another form of resource scarcity that leads institutionalized organizations to abandon costly traditions. For these reasons, we include a measure of the percentage change in membership from one year to the next in the analyses that follow.

Size and Age of Organizations

We include not only measures of the current economic and demographic condition of the kibbutzim, but also measures of several other enduring characteristics of these organizations, such as size and age. A number of theories suggest that the size and age of kibbutzim should influence their readiness to introduce these innovations, but the theories make differing predictions of the effects of these influences.

According to Michael Hannan and John Freeman's theory of organizational inertia (1984), all organizations grow less likely to change as they become older and larger. On the other hand, many of the innovations we are considering are changes that democratic and communal organizations have often been said to become more likely to introduce, the older and larger they become. In Max Weber's writings (1978), "direct democracy" in organizations transforms itself into bureaucracy as organizations age and grow. In the literature on producer cooperatives, this is the old idea that, similarly, cooperatives have a tendency to "degenerate" over time (Blumberg 1968; Mill 1909; Webb and Webb 1920).

Previous studies of kibbutzim and other cooperatives in Israel have often reported positive effects for both the age and size of organizations on the likelihood of departures from democratic traditions. In a study of the worker cooperatives in Israel's cities, such as the bus cooperatives, Raymond Russell and Robert Hanneman (1995) found these cooperatives to make more use of hired labor, the older and larger they became. In a study of forty-nine kibbutzim in the years 1976–1979, Menachem Rosner and Arnold Tannenbaum (1987) found that both the age and the size of a kibbutz had significantly negative effects on the rotation of officers; the age of the kibbutz also had a negative effect on participation in the assembly. On the basis of a survey of 636 kibbutz members conducted in 1991–1992, Eliezer Ben-Rafael (1997) reported that "in the older kibbutzim, members are more favorable to differential monetary rewarding and to privatization" (170), and that "the larger the kibbutz, the more it tends to be change-oriented" (172).

Eric Batstone (1983) argues that periods of degeneration in democratic workplaces are often followed by periods of regeneration, in which members reassert their democratic traditions. Degeneration followed by regeneration would produce a curvilinear effect for age on changes that take democratic workplaces away from their traditions, positive for low values of age and negative at higher values. Two studies of the use of nonmember labor in producer cooperatives have reported this type of effects for age. One dealt with French worker cooperatives (Estrin and Jones 1992). The other was Tal Simons and Paul Ingram's study (1997) of the use of hired labor in Israeli kibbutzim. To be sensitive to the possibility of similar curvilinear effects of age in this study, our models include both age and age-squared .

Distance from Cities

In her study of utopian communities in the United States, Rosabeth Kanter (1968) reported that communities that were geographically isolated and that avoided contact with outsiders were more likely than others to retain their communal structures for long periods. Regarding the kibbutzim, Avner Ben-Ner (1987) noted that kibbutzim that are near cities tend to become increasingly integrated into the urban market economy, and adopt increasingly individualistic patterns of consumption in response. In his survey of 636 kibbutz members conducted in 1991–1992, Ben-Rafael (1997) reported, "closeness to a city was found to be associated with a stronger support of differential monetary rewarding, commercialization of services, institutionalization of the public authority and businesslike management. . . . In brief, the proximity to urban centers does influence kibbutzniks to the sense of a wider support for changes which diminish the difference between kibbutz and city. This influence is more consistent than that of most other features of kibbutzim" (173–174).

Kibbutz Federations

In previous studies (Abramitzky 2008; Rosner and Tannenbaum 1987; Russell, Hanneman, and Getz 2006; Simons and Ingram 1997), kibbutzim affiliated with the smaller and more ideologically coherent Artzi federation have been found to be more faithful to kibbutz traditions in such areas as the avoidance of hired labor than the larger and more diverse Takam. We expect to find that Artzi kibbutzim were slower than Takam kibbutzim to adopt these innovations, as well.

Innovations Previously Adopted by the Kibbutz

The potential influences just mentioned are many, but not all, of the organizational characteristics likely to make one kibbutz more or less likely to introduce innovations than another. Kibbutzim also differ from one another in the average age of their members, and in the occupations, educations, and gender of their members. These differences contribute in turn to large differences among kibbutzim in the degree to which their members support or oppose reform (Ben-Rafael 1997; Palgi 1994, 2002).

Kibbutzim differ not only in the attitudes of members toward reform, but also in the ways they consider and implement reforms. Menachem Rosner and Shlomo Getz (1994, 42) note that in the past, changes arose in specific areas of specific kibbutzim, and "were the result of 'grass-roots' processes." In the 1990s, in contrast, "The treatment of change has become institutionalized. Many kibbutzim have set up committees whose job is to deal with changes, while in other kibbutzim existing committees perform this function. These bodies are not concerned with solving problems as they arise, but with suggesting and initiating changes to the kibbutz."

To capture differences among kibbutzim in the attitudes of their members toward reforms, and in the incidence of "innovation teams" (Near 1997, 352) and other structural elements that institutionalize the process of reform, our analyses include a count of the number of innovations already in use on the kibbutz.

Adoption of Innovations by Other Kibbutzim

In addition to taking into account the number of innovations previously adopted by a given kibbutz, we also take into consideration, in the analyses that follow, the number of kibbutzim that have previously adopted each change. The former information is relevant to predicting the readiness of an individual kibbutz to introduce change; the latter information should help in predicting which changes a reform-minded kibbutz will be most likely to introduce.

Paul DiMaggio and Walter W. Powell's (1983) theory of institutional isomorphism identifies three mechanisms that cause members of the same organizational field to resemble one another over time. One of these mechanisms is "mimetic isomorphism," which occurs when organizations imitate the practices of similar organizations in the face of uncertainty. Numerous studies have documented the spread of innovative practices in various organizational fields through such mimetic processes.

Differences among Innovations

The innovations being considered by the kibbutzim during this period differ from one another not only in the extent to which they have been accepted, but also in other ways. Some look like classic symptoms of degeneration and "decommunalization"; others may be signs of the regeneration (Batstone 1983) and reinstitutionalization (Jepperson 1991) of the kibbutz. Of the five sets of innovations discussed in chapter 2, the group labeled "new rights and entitlements" may be the strongest candidates for consideration as signs of democratic regeneration. The other four feature classic symptoms of degeneration and decommunalization: bureaucratization of decision making; increasing employment of and contact with nonmembers; privatization of consumption; and growing inequality in income. In the analyses shown in table A.3 and table A.4, we also consider how differences among these five categories affect the progress of innovations through the forms of deliberation and implementation shown in table 3.1.

The Deinstitutionalization of the Kibbutz

Models estimating the effects of all of these influences on transitions toward or away from use of these innovations are shown in tables A.3 and A.4. Here we summarize the most important results.

The findings presented in table A.3 and table A.4 provide at best only mixed support for predictions derived from theories of communal, cooperative, and democratic organizations. As in previous studies, isolated locations and membership in the more ideologically coherent Artzi federation make kibbutzim less likely to consider innovations. The effects of kibbutz age, size, and economic condition, however, are not consistent with expectations derived from this literature. It is not the older, larger, and more prosperous kibbutzim that are most likely to introduce innovations, but the kibbutzim that are most in need of resources.

Although theories of communes and labor-managed workplaces offer only limited help in explaining the decisions and actions taken by individual kibbutzim to adopt and implement these reforms, expectations derived from more general theories of organizations perform much better. As in Oliver's (1992) theory of "de-institutionalization," kibbutzim were led to adopt these reforms not by age, size, or increasing affluence, but by their need for economic and human resources. The kibbutzim did not grow into these changes; they were forced into them. The greater the organization's need for money or members, the more likely a kibbutz was to change.

Kibbutzim differ not only in their need for resources, but also in the readiness with which they resist or embrace change. Kibbutzim with high "organizational inertia" (Hannan and Freeman 1984) are not only less likely to consider change; they are also more likely to abandon changes after they have been accepted. As the number of changes previously adopted by a kibbutz increases, so does the likelihood of additional change.

Insofar as individual kibbutzim become motivated to make changes, in deciding which changes to introduce they are strongly influenced by examples set by other organizations of the same type. As shown in table A.3, the proportion of kibbutzim currently using an innovation is the only influence that exerts a consistently positive influence at every stage of consideration and implementation. This tendency of organizations to imitate similar organizations in the face of uncertainty is what Paul DiMaggio and Walter W. Powell (1983) describe as "mimetic isomorphism." As in Matthew Kraatz and Edward Zajac's (1996) analysis of "illegitimate" change, the reforms adopted by the kibbutzim in the 1990s arose not in strong organizations but in weak ones, and then spread through imitation to more successful kibbutzim.

The Uncertain Path to Kibbutz Reform

If we compare the earlier portions of this analysis to the later portions, a few common themes stand out. The first is that the reform of the kibbutzim is a long, multistage process. Kibbutzim rarely leap from "not considering" to currently "using" an innovation in a single year. More commonly, periods of deliberation and implementation are required before changes are introduced.

The process of change is divided into multiple stages, and different things happen at each stage. Each stage responds to a different set of causal influences, and each represents a different mix of hazards that can delay or derail the efforts at change. Innovations may be dropped from consideration or determined unworkable at any stage. The risk that innovations will be abandoned declines from stage to stage, but remains substantial even after innovations have been brought into use. Increases in the overall prevalence of innovations in the kibbutz population over time are, of course, the net effects of numerous transitions toward and away from use of innovations on individual kibbutzim.

Another common theme linking earlier portions of this analysis with later ones is that proposals to introduce inequality in compensation or ownership stand out as the most contentious and as the decisions most likely to be abandoned after reports that they had been accepted. In the 1990s, such problems limited differential compensation to small numbers of economically marginal kibbutzim. In the early years of the new century, however, increasing numbers of kibbutzim did adopt safety-net budgets, which in turn forced the kibbutz movement and the Israeli government to decide whether kibbutzim that paid differential salaries to members would still be entitled to call themselves kibbutzim. These two recent developments are described in chapter 4 and chapter 5.

4

Transformation of the Kibbutzim, 1995-2011

As we have shown in chapters 2 and 3, most kibbutzim made only modest reforms in the 1990s, and made even those changes with great hesitation. The great majority of kibbutzim introduced changes that did not violate traditional definitions of the kibbutzim codified in national laws and kibbutz bylaws, but avoided changes that explicitly contradicted these guidelines. The caution and indecisiveness with which the kibbutzim approached reform in this period were attributable not only to the difficulty of building lasting coalitions in favor of each change on individual kibbutzim, but also to the mixed signals that the kibbutzim received, during this period, from their federations regarding change. The federations promised the government and the banks that all kibbutzim would introduce reforms, but they simultaneously warned their members that if they started paying members differential, market-based salaries, they would be expelled from the kibbutz movement.

Despite these threats and other institutional obstacles, beginning in 1995, growing numbers of kibbutzim began to pay differential, market-based salaries to members. The number of such kibbutzim grew from a handful in the mid-1990s to 10 percent of all nonreligious kibbutzim by 1999, 25 percent by 2001. Since 2003, kibbutzim that pay differential salaries have outnumbered kibbutzim that continue to base household budgets solely on need.

Members of the kibbutzim that introduced this change were well aware that it was not just a new way to determine kibbutz members' incomes, but also a fundamental change in the relationship between the kibbutz and its members, and in the nature of the kibbutz. Unlike the reforms that most kibbutzim introduced in the 1990s, payment of differential salaries required a kibbutz to amend the definition of a kibbutz contained in its own bylaws, in ways that contradicted the definitions of a kibbutz approved by the federations and codified in Israeli law.

In chapter 4, we examine how individual kibbutzim made the decision to pay differential salaries to members, during the years between 1995 and 2005. We begin by describing the invention and spread of the so-called safety-net budgetary system, which within less than ten years would displace need-based budgeting on a growing majority of kibbutzim. In later sections, we identify additional changes that often accompany payment of differential salaries, and estimate the effects of a number of potential influences on the likelihood that an individual kibbutz would introduce this change, during the years between 1995 and 2005. How the kibbutz federations and Israeli government reacted to this change in the identity of the kibbutzim, we take up in chapter 5.

Redefining the Ownership of the Kibbutzim

In chapters 2 and 3, we have shown that, in the 1990s, proposals to change compensation or ownership in a kibbutz were less likely than other reforms to be adopted, and were more likely than other reforms to be rejected or to be abandoned after initially being approval. The reluctance of individual kibbutzim to adopt these proposals was due not only to the inherently controversial nature of the reforms, but also to the fact that they explicitly contradicted the bylaws of the kibbutzim. Whereas most reforms of the 1990s could be adopted by majority vote, proposals to amend kibbutz bylaws required the support of three-quarters of the members.

The model bylaws disseminated by the kibbutz federations in the 1970s stipulated in several ways that kibbutz members as individuals did not and could not own any assets separable from the collective property of the kibbutzim. Article 53 required kibbutz members to transfer all of their property to the kibbutz at the time they become members. Article 42 declared, "The kibbutz has no share capital. The kibbutz member has no capital rights whatsoever in the kibbutz" (Yassour 1977, 331). Article 44 stated that "the kibbutz property is not distributable among its members, neither during its existence nor upon its liquidation" (Yassour 1977, 331). Before kibbutzim could pay members' salaries into individually owned bank accounts, or issue shares of stock in kibbutz ventures to their members, they would first need to amend some or all of these bylaws.

In 1995, the kibbutz federations notified their member kibbutzim that some bylaw provisions regarding the ownership of kibbutz assets had been rendered obsolete by the financial crisis of the 1980s and now needed to be changed. Although the land on which most kibbutzim are located is owned by the kibbutzim, ownership of the movable assets of the kibbutzim such as vehicles, farm equipment, and machinery was vested, since 1926, in a cooperative holding company called Nir (Shapiro 1976, 133–134). The model kibbutz bylaws disseminated in the 1970s stipulated that the kibbutz was a member of Nir, and that in the event of liquidation, the surplus assets of the kibbutz would be transferred to Nir. Because Nir had become bankrupt in the 1980s, the kibbutz movement advised the kibbutzim in 1995 to amend their bylaws to delete the Nir provisions.

Although these amendments might have struck some observers and participants as purely technical, the deletion of provisions regarding Nir from kibbutz bylaws contributed in a number of ways to the larger changes soon to follow. Although the exercise may have reminded kibbutz members of the barriers to change presented by the bylaws, it also showed that bylaws could be amended. By making the kibbutz rather than Nir the owner of kibbutz capital assets, these amendments gave kibbutz members powerful incentives to make additional amendments to privatize these collective assets.

Invention and Spread of the Safety-Net Budget

In the early 1990s, Kibbutz Ein Zivan and Kibbutz Snir became the first kibbutzim to announce that they intended to pay differential salaries to members, but they were slow to put these plans into practice. The kibbutz federations threatened to expel any kibbutz that followed through on such plans, making other kibbutzim even more reluctant to take this step.

Beginning around 1995, Kibbutz Gesher Haziv and Kibbutz Naot Mordechai found a way to make payment of differential salaries more palatable to kibbutz members. They created the so-called safety-net budget, in which members would receive differential, market-based salaries but would have their incomes taxed progressively to support a minimal standard of living and level of social services for all kibbutz members. The safety-net budget sounded more like Scandinavian socialism than like capitalism, making it a less radical departure from the traditional political culture of the kibbutzim. Politically, by using taxes collected from healthy working-aged members to meet the needs of older and weaker members, the safety-net budgetary system had the potential to create alliances between the two.

Attaining the high level of support required to make a transformation of this magnitude was not easy. Debates over the future of a kibbutz could become bitter, with members on both sides threatening to leave the kibbutz if the vote went against them. Gaining the 75 percent support required for approval required the creation of broad coalitions, uniting managers who wanted to use differential pay as an incentive with seniors who sought assurance that the height of the so-called safety net would not be set too low. A consultant told Daniel Gavron regarding one kibbutz that "the process of change there is unbelievably complex. In a business you have to convince one manager and maybe six board members. In a kibbutz you have to convince 75 percent of the community" (Gavron 2000, 93).

In many kibbutzim, members have been unable to reach agreement about which course to take, without the assistance of outside experts, or managers hired to serve as "change agents." Some of the earliest instances of the safety-net budget emerged under the leadership of influential figures of this sort, such as Israel Tsufim and Israel Oz. It was Tsufim who, while working with Kibbutz Gesher Haziv, first came up with the idea of calling the new system a safety-net budget. For Tsufim, this label was not just a way to make unequal pay more acceptable to kibbutz members; it also involved a new system of taxation for the kibbutz, and a new way of thinking about the responsibilities that kibbutz members owed to one another.

Tsufim's system begins with a community tax that covers municipal services like refuse collection, and is the same for everyone. It then adds a "balancing tax," which is based on net family income. The balancing tax is paid on the net income of families whose income exceeds the minimum cost of living defined by the Israeli government. The amounts collected through the balancing tax are used to subsidize the incomes of kibbutz members whose earnings would otherwise fall below the minimum set by the government. That is the sense in which the balancing tax provides members with a so-called safety net.

Another early architect of the safety-net budget was Israel Oz at Kibbutz Naot Mordechai. In 1989, Oz was one of the government officials who insisted that the kibbutzim must pledge themselves to make reforms before they could emerge from bankruptcy. After he left the government, Oz became an advocate of the privatization of the kibbutzim, and began to publish recommendations. Oz now argues that, in Tsufim's model, the community tax is too high and is effectively regressive. Oz favors a low community tax, coupled with a tax based on personal incomes rather than on family incomes, and that is high and progressive.

Both Tsufim and Oz were each personally involved in several of the earliest instances of the safety-net budget, and consulting firms that they founded have assisted in many more. In a personal interview conducted in his office in Tel Aviv in July of 2008, Oz estimated that perhaps as many as fifty, sixty, or seventy kibbutzim had made their transitions with the help of Israel Tsufim and his associates, and another ten to twelve had been advised by his own firm.

Tsufim and Oz use very different approaches to transform a kibbutz. Oz expects a kibbutz to agree to his proposals at the start, and then to hire him or one of his associates to manage the kibbutz during the period of transition. Tsufim acts as an outside consultant, and invests time to develop a consensus that may be unique to each kibbutz. One consultant told us in 2008 that what kibbutzim look for from consultants is not a matter of specific solutions, but rather guidance with the ideological and symbolic aspects of change. The process of transformation had, he said, to be presented to the members in a vocabulary that would point to the justifications for the change.

In the late 1990s and early years of the new century, increasing numbers of kibbutzim began to follow Tsufim's or Oz's recommendations, or to pursue similar ideas of their own. Many kibbutzim also began to experiment with so-called mixed models, of which Tsufim had been one of the most prominent advocates in the early 1990s.

Transitions among Types of Budgets, 1995–2011

The number of kibbutzim adopting safety-net or mixed budgets in each year since 1995 is shown in table 4.1. In the earliest years, with the kibbutz federations and the Registrar of Cooperatives threatening to expel from the movement any kibbutz that paid differential salaries to its members, the mixed model struck many kibbutz members as a much safer compromise. Between 1996 and 2000, the number of kibbutzim adopting mixed systems of compensation exceeded, in each year, the number of kibbutzim adopting safety-net budgets (table 4.1).

In the 1990s, some advocates of mixed systems of compensation viewed the mixed model not just as a compromise, but as a viable alternative

TABLE 4.1.

Transitions among Types of Budget, 1995–2011

Year	Need-based to mixed	Need-based to safety-net	Mixed to safety-net
1995	1	2	0
1996	6	3	0
1997	9	5	1
1998	10	6	1
1999	7	6	1
2000	13	11	5
2001	10	14	10
2002	7	20	13
2003	3	9	5
2004	7	13	4
2005	2	7	12
2006	1	3	3
2007	0	7	5
2008	2	5	5
2009	0	3	2
2010	1	1	2
2011	0	1	2
Total	79	116	71

to the traditional and safety-net budgets. Beginning in the year 2000, however, increasing numbers of kibbutzim with mixed forms of payment abandoned the remaining traditional elements in their compensation and adopted fully differential systems. In most years since 2001, the number of mixed kibbutzim adopting safety-net budgets has exceeded the number of traditional kibbutzim adopting mixed budgets, causing the total number of kibbutzim with mixed systems to decline.

The traditional kibbutz and the differential kibbutz each seem to adhere to a coherent institutional logic. Kibbutzim of the mixed type, on the other hand, are hybrid organizations. Heather Haveman and Hyagreeva Rao (2006, 974) describe hybrid organizations as those that "combine the institutional logics that are materialized in two or more organizational forms." Where institutional logics are combined, they may come into conflict; this seems especially likely in the mixed kibbutzim, which explicitly mix principles of compensation that are diametrically opposed.

For kibbutzim of the mixed type, the formation of a clear organizational identity has been especially difficult, because most organizations adopting this model do not do so out of any conviction that the mixed model is superior to its alternatives. It is adopted in reaction to internal stalemate between members supporting transformation and those against it, not because members are inspired by the possibility of creating a hybrid or intermediate organizational form. In the mid-1990s, the consultant Israel Tsufim briefly attempted to develop a so-called mixed model, but soon went on to create the safety-net budget.

Raymond Russell, Robert Hanneman, and Shlomo Getz (2011, 114) estimate that, in the five years from 2000 through 2004, a quarter to a third of all kibbutzim with mixed compensation systems adopted fully differential budgets in each year. Few kibbutzim retained mixed compensation systems for more than two or three years, and only new adoptions of the mixed form by additional kibbutzim in every year kept this category from disappearing. Given the short duration of the mixed form of compensation, this type is best viewed not as an alternative to the safety-net budget but as a "transitional identity" (Clark et al. 2010) serving as an indirect path to the same end—namely, the safety-net mode. Although the mixed form has proved short-lived, its importance should not be underestimated. More than a third of all kibbutzim with safety-net budgets in 2011 took their first steps away from need-based compensation by using mixed forms of compensation during transitional periods of two to four years.

No kibbutz that has made the transition from either need-based or mixed-compensation to safety-net budgeting has ever abandoned its differential salary system in favor of returning to need-based or mixed compensation. Adopting differential compensation requires the kibbutzim making this change to amend their bylaws so as to make individual members, rather than the kibbutz as a whole, the owner of kibbutz assets. Participants in these decisions are well aware that these new forms of compensation signify a fundamental change in the identity of the kibbutz, and typically spend years preparing for the change, often with the help of consultants and special committees. Once three-quarters of the members of a kibbutz have approved a transformation and that change has been incorporated into the relevant written documents, the change cannot easily be undone. When the change has taken assets previously owned by the kibbutz and made them the property of the individual members, it would be especially difficult to put these assets together again.

Other Reforms in Kibbutzim with Differential Payment

By the final year of the Institute's annual surveys of innovations in 2001, kibbutzim with safety-net or mixed budgets had differentiated themselves from the traditional kibbutzim in a number of significant ways. In these kibbutzim, privatization had been taken much further than in kibbutzim that continued to base household budgets on need. In addition to requiring members to pay for electricity, meals, and travel, these kibbutzim had also privatized laundry and health services, recreation, and education, and had cancelled the morning meal in their dining halls. Most also reported that they were in favor of separating the economy from the community, treating economic branches as profit centers, and outsourcing services.

By 2002, kibbutzim with safety-net budgets had become so widely differentiated from traditional kibbutzim that the Institute decided to split its annual survey into separate surveys of kibbutzim of each kind, traditional (or mixed) and safety-net. One motivation for this was to observe forms of behavior that were emerging on the safety-net kibbutzim that had no counterparts on the traditional kibbutzim. Even where the same question could still be asked of kibbutzim of both types, the answers given took on entirely different meanings in the differing contexts. In the case of paying for meals in the dining hall, for example, if a traditional kibbutz reported that it was "not considering" this reform, the answer meant that members continued to eat in its dining hall for free. By 2006, about 50 percent of kibbutzim with safety-net budgets had closed their dining halls, and on these kibbutzim, members did not pay for meals because the kibbutz provided no meals; in this context, "not considering" charging members for meals in the dining hall meant that members were eating on their own and had to purchase food somewhere else.

In addition to closing their dining halls, many kibbutzim that pay differential salaries have also closed their laundries, and have privatized many more expenses previously shared by the communal household in such areas as education and health care. Medical expenses being privatized include costs of health insurance, medications, dental care, psychological counseling, and travel for medical treatment. Educational expenses now being paid by members include special and extracurricular education for children, and higher educational expenses of the members themselves. And, on these kibbutzim, celebrations of events such as a Bar Mitzvah or a wedding, previously treated as communal occasions, are now being treated as expenses of individual families.

According to Roger Friedland and Robert Alford (1991), adhering to a common institutional logic gives organizations both internal coherence and external legitimacy. The logics available to organizations emanate from major institutions of a society, such as the polity or the economy. The polity, for example, may be organized around the principle of democracy, even while the economy may be organized around the principle of rationality or efficiency.

Although the architects of the safety-net kibbutz had no common theory, they shared an agenda of replacing kibbutz approaches to problems and decisions with more conventional business solutions and practices. Moreover, if managerial positions in kibbutzim were to be opened to non-members, they needed to be described in terms that would be meaningful and attractive to managers coming from outside. All of this has given a striking logical coherence to the changes that kibbutzim with market-based salaries have made in the terminology used to refer to job titles and functions, as shown in table 4.2.

TABLE 4.2.

Organizational Titles in Traditional and Differential Kibbutzim

Traditional kibbutzim	Differential kibbutzim
Mazkir	*Menahel Kehilah*
Secretary	Manager of the community
Mesader Avodah; Sadran Avodah	*Menahel Mashabei Enosh*
Arranger of work; Labor coordinator	Manager of human resources
Anaf	*Esek*
Branch	Business
Ekonom	*Menahel Anaf Mazon*
Head of kitchen and dining hall	Manager of food branch
Merakez Meshek	*Yoshev Rosh Moetset Menahalim; Menahel Asakim*
Coordinator of the economy	Chairman of the board of directors; business manager

The traditional kibbutz clearly takes its inspiration from the political ideals of democracy and equality. As in many socialist political parties, the leading executive figure is described only as a *secretary*. Each agricultural or industrial venture is viewed as a *branch* or part of a collective and centrally planned economy. Heads of branches or other activities are called *coordinators* or *organizers*, not *managers*.

The market-oriented kibbutz, in contrast, systematically replaces this egalitarian and collectivist vocabulary with the terminology of managerial capitalism. The kibbutz secretary is replaced by a *manager of the community*. What was once called a *branch* is now called a *business*. The *labor coordinator* has been replaced by a manager of human resources. Activities that were formerly under the control of a *committee* are now under the control of a *management* or *board of directors*.

Just as seen in the work of Friedland and Alford (1991) and of later researchers (Marquis and Lounsbury 2007; Thornton 2002; Zilber 2002), institutional logics are not independent of the political and economic forces that advocate and enact them. The vocabulary of the transformed kibbutzim has clear roots in the new liberalism of the 1980s, which inspired Israeli politics during the period of kibbutz reform. By adopting this terminology, the kibbutzim improved their fit with their environment. This is also why the term *privatization*, which in the 1990s referred only to changes in consumption, is now being applied to the entire transformation.

Within the kibbutzim, the adoption of this new terminology to describe managerial positions represents the ideological ascendancy of the technocrats (Topel 2005). Whereas, in the 1990s, most kibbutzim continued to reject many aspects of the managers' program, the vocabulary of kibbutzim that pay differential salaries frankly acknowledges the importance to the kibbutz of the specialized work of its administrative staff.

By illustrating the extent to which need-based and differential budgets each reflect distinct and coherent institutional logics, table 4.2 sheds new light on the transitory nature of the mixed kibbutz that was shown in table 4.1. It is tempting to attribute the lower stability of the mixed kibbutzim to the fact that they seek to incorporate two explicitly contradictory institutional logics (Marquis and Lounsbury 2007; Seo and Creed 2002; Thornton 2002).

Influences on Transformations

In table A.7 in the appendix, we estimate the effects of a number of potential influences on the likelihood that individual kibbutzim would adopt mixed or safety-net budgets in the years from 1995 through 2005.

Just as it was in regard to diffusion of changes between 1990 and 2001, the literature on democratic and communal organizations is of mixed value as a guide to understanding these recent transformations in the kibbutzim. As this literature leads us to expect, kibbutzim that belong to the more ideologically committed Artzi federation, or that are situated in geographically isolated locations such as the Negev, have been less likely than other kibbutzim to abandon need-based budgeting in favor of mixed or safety-net compensation. There is also some evidence that the age of a kibbutz has the curvilinear effect that Eric Batstone (1987) predicts. This finding, however, attains statistical significance only in the case of transformations from need-based to mixed forms of compensation.

When we turn our attention to the effects of the size and the economic condition of a kibbutz, here as in the previous chapter the effects of these influences is not at all what the work of authors like Max Weber (1978) and Rosabeth Kanter (1968) suggests. The kibbutzim that were most likely to adopt new forms of compensation over the ten years beginning in 1995 were not the larger and more prosperous kibbutzim, but the organizations that were smaller and weaker than others.

Although theories of democratic and communal organizations are of only mixed utility in explaining these recent changes in the identity of the kibbutzim, more general theories of change in organizations do much better. Of the general organizational influences tested here, the most prominent role is once again played by resources.

Some accounts of the problems that prompted the recent waves of changes in the kibbutzim describe the crisis of the kibbutzim as if it were an event that occurred in the 1980s and ended soon after the kibbutzim emerged from collective bankruptcy. But the fiscal and demographic problems of the kibbutzim persisted throughout the 1990s, and well into the new century. Tables A.3 and A.6 indicate that the average economic and demographic condition of the kibbutzim remained as bad during the ten years in which safety-net budgets and mixed forms of compensation were initially spreading (1995–2004) as they had been during the first decade of innovation. During these years, the average kibbutz had 218 members, and was losing an average of 1.6 members per year.

Models of the adoption of mixed and safety-net budgets shown in table A.7 indicate that economic problems on individual kibbutzim made those kibbutzim more likely to make every kind of transformation: from need-based budgets to mixed compensation, from need-based to safety-net budgets, and from mixed compensation to safety-net budgets. Loss of members, on the other hand, made kibbutzim with need-based budgets more likely to adopt mixed compensation, but had no significant effect on the adoption of safety-net budgets. Given that the mixed form of compensation is inherently a compromise, it is not surprising to find that this form is particularly attractive to the demographically weaker kibbutzim. It is the kibbutzim that are losing the most members that have the greatest need to try to please everyone.

In addition to being highly responsive to resource scarcity, the diffusion of new forms of compensation among the kibbutzim has also strongly associated with the inertia of individual organizations, and the examples set by other organizations of the same kind. In these analyses of forms of compensation, as in the previous analyses of the diffusion of the larger set of innovations, the most pervasive influences on change in the kibbutzim are the organization's prior experience with change, and the examples set by other kibbutzim previously introducing the same change. In both analyses, general processes of resource dependence, organizational inertia, and institutional isomorphism appear more salient to the recent changes in the kibbutzim than theories that stress the unique nature of kibbutzim as democratic or communal organizations.

Conclusions

In chapters 2 and 3, we watched the kibbutzim gradually introduce a large number of small changes. They adopted reforms that had been approved by their federations and that large numbers of other kibbutzim were also adopting, while avoiding radical changes.

In chapter 4, we have seen growing numbers of kibbutzim make a much more far-reaching change, one that completely transformed the identity of the organizations adopting it. The transformative nature of this change in compensation has been evident throughout this chapter, in many ways. The payment of market-based salaries to kibbutz members brought with it a large number of additional changes, as well as a new worldview and institutional logic. That these innovations were altering the organization's core identity was made explicit for participants when kibbutz members voted to codify the changes through amendments to their bylaws. Data on year-to-year transitions among forms of compensation indicate that the adoption of differential salaries by a kibbutz is a transformation from which there is no turning back.

The change in compensation described in chapter 4 was different in many ways from the reforms that preceded it. Whereas the reforms of the 1990s were introduced by hesitant, unstable majorities and were often quickly abandoned, decisions by kibbutzim to begin paying differential salaries to their members were consensual and permanent.

Although the adoption of differential compensation by the kibbutzim was a much more radical and transformative change than the earlier reforms, it was not unrelated to them. Privatization of consumption on kibbutzim was a necessary precondition for differential salaries to be effective as incentives, and the successful introduction of modest reforms helped the kibbutzim to overcome their "organizational inertia" and institutionalize the process of change.

From just two kibbutzim in 1995, the safety-net budget had spread by 1999 to twenty-five kibbutzim, representing 10 percent of the total. By 2002, kibbutzim with safety-net or mixed systems of compensation outnumbered kibbutzim that continued to base household budgets solely on need. It was clear to everyone involved that the kibbutzim affected had been greatly transformed by this change, but neither the kibbutz movement nor the government had yet followed through on threats to expel kibbutzim that paid differential salaries from the movement.

How the kibbutz movement and the Israeli government reacted to the widespread adoption of the safety-net budget is the subject of chapter 5. In concluding chapter 4, it is worthwhile to add that, during the years in which the safety-net budget rose from obscurity to become the predominant organizational form in the kibbutz population, it had many characteristics of what Matthew Kraatz and Edward Zajac (1996) have labeled an *illegitimate change*. From 1995 until well into the next century, payment of differential salaries by kibbutzim contradicted both the written policies of their federations and legal definitions of the kibbutzim. Like the so-called illegitimate changes in undergraduate curricula described by Kraatz and Zajac (1996), market-based salaries originated in kibbutzim that were most in need of resources, and then spread through imitation from the weak organizations to the strong. Whatever legitimation this innovation would later receive from the kibbutz movement and Israeli government would come long after the majority of kibbutzim had already committed themselves to adopt the new organizational identity.

5

From Transformation to Renewal

By the early years of the new century, kibbutzim that paid differential salaries to members were becoming more numerous than kibbutzim that continued to base household budgets on need. The kibbutzim that made this change had clearly been greatly transformed by it, but what they had transformed themselves into was not yet clear.

In chapter 5, we begin with the response of the kibbutz movement and the Israeli government to the growing popularity of the safety-net budget in the years after 2002. That discussion led by 2005 to an official acknowledgment that kibbutzim paying differential salaries were still kibbutzim, but kibbutzim of a new type, the so-called renewed kibbutz. In later sections of chapter 5, we consider the implications of this transformation for other aspects of the organizational identity of the kibbutzim, including the extent to which the kibbutzim still merit consideration as democratic, cooperative, and communal organizations, and the extent to which they continue to share a common organizational identity of any kind.

Still a Kibbutz?

When individual kibbutzim first began to adopt differential compensation in the 1990s, leaders of the federations warned them that any kibbutz making this change would no longer be considered a kibbutz. The Registrar of Cooperative Societies issued similar threats. In the years following these transformations, however, neither the federations nor the Registrar took action.

In 1999, eight members of Kibbutz Beit Oren finally forced the Israeli government to take a stand on this question, when they asked the Supreme Court sitting as the High Court of Justice to instruct the Registrar of Cooperative Societies to end the classification of Beit Oren as a kibbutz. Beit Oren had introduced differential salaries, closed its communal dining hall, and privatized education and other services, making it in the eyes of the petitioners no longer a kibbutz. Cases such as this led the government of Israel to decide, in February 2002, to form a public committee to examine the question. The Public Committee on the Issue of Kibbutzim, chaired by sociologist Eliezer Ben-Rafael of Tel Aviv University, issued its report in 2003.

When Ben-Rafael's Public Committee began its work, a kibbutz was defined in Israel's Cooperative Societies Ordinance as "a cooperative society that is a separate settlement, organized on the basis of collective ownership of assets, self-employment, equality and cooperation in production, consumption, and education." The Public Committee recommended that this wording be retained as the definition of a "collective" or "communal" kibbutz, and that a second definition should be added for the "renewing" (Ben-Rafael and Topel 2011) or "renewed" (Manor 2004) kibbutz. A renewed kibbutz would be defined as:

a cooperative society that is a separate settlement, organized on the basis of collective partnership in assets, self-employment, equality and cooperation in production, consumption, and education, that maintains mutual responsibility among its members, and whose articles of association include some or all of the following:

(1) Relative wages according to individual contribution or seniority;

(2) Allocation of apartments;

(3) Allocation of means of production to its members, excluding land, water and production quotas, provided that the cooperative maintains control over the means of production and that its articles of association restrict the negotiability of allocated means of production. (Manor 2004)

Some authors were quick to express skepticism about whether a renewed kibbutz really deserved to be called a kibbutz. According to Ronen Manor (2004),

In our opinion, most kibbutzim fail to meet even the new definition of Renewed Kibbutz, because there is no equality among members—not in their revenues, not in their consumption, nor in their production. Kibbutzim pay differential wages, and in their search for cheap labor they prefer to employ outsiders and not kibbutz members, meaning that even the value of self-employment is disregarded. Furthermore, due to the drastic cutbacks in community services, not much remains of the mutual guarantee principle, and members increasingly need to rely on themselves.

Despite such criticisms, both the kibbutz movement and the Israeli government quickly accepted the recommendations of the Public Committee, and they became law in October 2005. In The distribution of kibbutzim by type (using the definitions provided in this law), from 1995 through 2011, is shown in table 5.1. In the eyes of the law, kibbutzim with mixed forms of compensation are classified with collective kibbutzim, but we follow the practice of other researchers in providing separate counts of this type. By 2011, the number of kibbutzim following the so-called mixed model had fallen from a peak of thirty-seven in the years 2000 and 2001 to just seven. The renewed form of kibbutzim, as already noted, had become the predominant type of kibbutz several years before it gained legal recognition as a kibbutz.

Even though the definitions crafted by Ben-Rafael's Public Committee have helped to hold the kibbutz population together in the short term, they may not continue to do so indefinitely. The amount of mutual responsibility that members accept on each kibbutz, and the limits of that responsibility, are now much discussed questions on all kibbutzim. Insofar as the height of the safety net comes to vary significantly between one kibbutz and another, this feature could someday come to divide the kibbutzim as much as it now helps to unite them.

One sign of continued uncertainty regarding the organizational identity of renewed kibbutzim is that there is as yet no standardized terminology in Hebrew or English for referring to them. In this work, we follow the recommendation of Ben-Rafael's Public Committee in labeling all kibbutzim that pay differential salaries renewed kibbutzim. In surveys conducted by the Institute for Research of the Kibbutz at the University of

TABLE 5.1.

Kibbutzim by Type, 1995–2011

	Collective	Mixed	Renewed	Total
1995	247	0	2	249
1996	238	6	5	249
1997	223	15	11	249
1998	207	24	18	249
1999	194	30	25	249
2000	171	37	41	249
2001	146	37	66	249
2002	120	32	97	249
2003	107	31	111	249
2004	89	32	128	249
2005	76	24	149	249
2006	73	19	156	248
2007	66	16	166	248
2008	58	12	178	248
2009	55	10	183	248
2010	54	9	185	248
2011	53	7	188	248

Haifa, kibbutzim that pay differential salaries to members have been designated, since 1990 as differential kibbutzim (e.g., Palgi and Orchan 2007, 2011). The kibbutz movement formally endorsed the recommendations of the Public Committee in 2004, but its Annual Reports continued to list kibbutzim that pay differential salaries as safety-net kibbutzim (Arbel 2005, 2006). Kibbutz members now most frequently describe their kibbutz as being "privatized," and the Israeli media also follow this practice.

Kibbutzim as Alternative Organizations

In addition to throwing into question the right of kibbutzim to continue to call themselves kibbutzim, the recent changes in them have also strained their identities as communes, as cooperatives, and as democratic organizations. In this section, we discuss the extent to which each of these three labels continues to apply to the kibbutzim.

Kibbutzim as Communes

Every step in the privatization of the kibbutz has simultaneously been a step in its decommunalization. Although privatization has gone far since 1990, it has so far been confined to the sphere of consumption. Activities that bring revenue into the kibbutz, such as agriculture and manufacturing, often have external partners, but kibbutz members' stakes in these enterprises continue to be collectively owned. Even when kibbutzim transfer shares of stock in profitable subsidiaries to individual kibbutz members, Eliezer Ben-Rafael and Menachem Topel (2009, ix) note, "members are allotted shares that represent their part in the collective capital invested in factories, agricultural crops, and other productive activities. Here, kibbutz branches remain organized on the basis of collective sharing that binds the settlement's membership." The kibbutz economy is therefore still a communal economy, and the kibbutzim continue to merit attention as communes.

Table 5.2 shows the distribution of kibbutz residents by status, over the years 1998 through 2010. The total number of kibbutz members declined from 53,844 in 1998 to 50,268 in 2010, an average loss of 1.2 members per kibbutz per year. The number of children living on kibbutzim fell during these years from 29,127 to 17,979, declining by more than a third. What prevented the total kibbutz population from declining during these years was the growth of various categories of nonmember. Kibbutz-born adults who were not members of the kibbutz rose from 8,631 in 1998 to 10,310 in 2003, the last year for which this figure is available. Temporary residents of kibbutzim rose from 13,236 in 1998 to 35,639 in 2010, while a new category, "other permanent residents," was responsible for another 19,983 adults in 2010.

The explosive growth in these two categories of nonmembers reflects decisions made by most kibbutzim in the 1990s to rent housing on kibbutzim to nonmembers, and by some kibbutzim to sell houses to nonmembers. Nonmembers renting housing on kibbutzim were classified as temporary residents; the category includes students in nearby colleges as well as families renting entire houses. By 2010, more than eighty kibbutzim had opened new neighborhoods in which nonmembers could buy houses or erect their own

TABLE 5.2.

Kibbutz Population by Status, 1998–2010

Status	1998	2000	2002	2004	2006	2008	2010
Members	53,844	50,855	52,620	52,277	52,583	50,891	50,268
Soldiers	4,122	4,188	3,861	3,948	3,720	3,151	2,950
Kibbutz-born	8,631	7,968	10,249	NA	NA	NA	NA
Candidates and others	2,169	1,990	1,807	5,424	4,535	3,841	2,653
Parents and relatives	1,171	981	1,004	879	717	606	540
Other permanent residents	0	0	7,036	15,040	16,240	16,933	19,983
Total adults	69,937	65,982	76,577	77,568	77,795	75,422	76,394
Children	29,127	26,333	23,882	21,741	20,154	18,490	17,979
Total permanent residents	99,064	94,504	100,459	99,309	97,949	93,912	94,373
Temporary residents	13,236	14,940	11,410	11,516	17,038	30,216	35,639
Total children	112,300	109,444	111,869	110,825	114,987	124,128	130,012
Religious kibbutzim	6,000	5,856	6,838	6,822	7,760	9,672	10,888
Total kibbutz population	118,300	115,300	118,707	117,647	122,747	133,800	140,900

Source: Arbel 2004, 2005, 2006; Yoffe 2004; Shulamit Arbel, personal communication, 2008 & 2010

homes, and another seventy kibbutzim were planning such neighborhoods (Charney and Palgi 2011, 260); permanent residents would be nonmembers who lived in these neighborhoods and bought or built their own house.

Although the number of members on kibbutzim has declined, temporary and permanent residents together now constitute the majority of the adults living on kibbutzim. When a kibbutz member walks across a kibbutz today, most of the faces he or she encounters are those of nonmembers—hired employees of the kibbutz, people who rent housing from the kibbutz, or persons who have come by to drop off or pick up children, or to buy food in the kibbutz's grocery store. In the kibbutz, as in the society outside it, interactions among strangers have become more frequent than contact between members of the collective household (Getz 1998b).

Kibbutzim as Cooperatives

The kibbutzim also continue to be registered with the Israeli government as cooperatives, although they clearly become less cooperative with each passing year. By 2004, 24,000, or 35.3 percent of all kibbutz members and other adult residents, commuted to jobs outside the kibbutz. Of the 86,800 employed in the kibbutz economy that year, 44,500, or 51.3 percent, were nonmembers (Pavin 2007, 9)

Although a kibbutz is still marginally a cooperative, it is no longer a "whole cooperative," as Martin Buber (1958) described it, uniting both production and consumption in the same entity. Today's kibbutz economy is focused on production, and consumption on today's kibbutzim has been turned over to private decisions made by individual households.

Changes in Kibbutz Democracy

As the kibbutzim have become less communal and less cooperative, they have also become less democratic. Employees and residents who are not members of the kibbutz are excluded from many decisions. Members have also transferred control of economic ventures from the General Assembly of members to autonomous boards of directors.

Although kibbutz democracy has acquired new limitations and has made important concessions, the kibbutzim have not given up their democratic practices so readily or so completely as they have abandoned many aspects of their communal and cooperative identities. Some reforms of the 1990s, such as voting by secret ballot, were seen at the time as ways to strengthen kibbutz democracy. Throughout that decade, most kibbutzim showed little interest in reforms that would transfer the authority of the General Assembly to a representative council, or that would allow holders of managerial offices to keep their jobs when their terms expired. Members have continued to vote on all major decisions, including election of officers, admission of new members, approval of the annual budget, and major changes in the way of life of the kibbutz.

Because proposals for change require the support of a majority or more of the members, the process of change has given rank-and-file kibbutz members and threatened minorities, such as seniors, the power to veto proposed changes by managers. In chapter 3, we showed that the reforms most widely adopted in the 1990s were those that increased the autonomy, rights, and security of individual kibbutz members; the least popular reforms, on the other hand, included many that reflected a more narrowly managerial agenda.

Influences on Transformations

We have seen the kibbutzim become less communal, less cooperative, and less democratic over time, as theories of the transformation of such organizations predict. But the influences that seem most responsible for producing these transformations are not the influences that theories of developmental communalism, cooperative degeneration, and the transformation of direct democracy customarily point toward.

In the work of Max Weber (1978), for example, the transformation of direct democracy into bureaucracy comes about in response to a number of internal developments: growing organizational size, advancing age, and increasing technical complexity. In this study, we have found internal organizational conditions of this sort to be less influential than a number of external influences, such as whether a kibbutz is gaining or losing material and human resources in its exchanges with its environment.

While this study has provided little support for theories that attribute the transformation of communal and democratic organizations to internal processes, it is more consistent with studies giving more emphasis to how these organizations relate to their environments. Just as Rosabeth Kanter (1968) found in her work, for example, we find that kibbutzim in isolated locations are more likely than others to retain collective practices. And, like Menachem Rosner and Arnold Tannenbaum (1987) and Tal Simons and Paul Ingram (1997), we find that kibbutzim that, until the recent merger, belonged to the more ideologically coherent Artzi Federation are less likely to introduce reforms of any type. Given the central role played in the kibbutzim's changes by economic and demographic crisis, our findings are also consistent with previous studies that attribute change to dependencies on external markets. Within the kibbutz literature, this interpretation is illustrated by the work of Haim Barkai (1977) and Tal Simons and Paul Ingram (1997).

Kibbutzim as Organizations

The kibbutzim hold tenuously to their traditional identities as communal, cooperative, and democratic organizations; however, this analysis has found that several universal processes affecting most or all organizations to have been more relevant to the kibbutzim's recent transformation than have any of these ways in which they have been considered unique. Like other organizations, kibbutzim depend on material and human resources, and they become more likely to abandon costly traditions to the extent that either sort of resources becomes scarce. Like other organizations, individual kibbutzim differ in the readiness with which they embrace or resist change. In 1990, all kibbutzim had high levels of organizational inertia, but within a decade, individual kibbutzim were accumulating increasing experience with change, and the organizational field as a whole was producing increasing numbers of consultants and institutional entrepreneurs. Finally, like other organizations, the kibbutzim were heavily influenced by other organizations from the same population in deciding which changes to adopt.

In the sections that follow, we offer a few additional comments on each of these themes.

From Crisis to Transformation

One theme links several chapters in this book. The kibbutz began, in 1990, with high levels of organizational inertia, but, over time, the needs of these organizations for material and human resources proved stronger than their loyalty to their traditions. In 1989, the government required the kibbutzim to agree to introduce reforms as one of the conditions of their emergence from bankruptcy, and the kibbutzim pledged themselves to do so. Individual kibbutzim were left free to choose which reforms they would and would not introduce, but for kibbutzim that were in trouble with creditors, doing nothing was no longer an option.

As the previous chapters have indicated, the crisis that inspired the recent series of changes in the kibbutzim was not limited to the 1980s. The kibbutzim remained economically and demographically stagnant throughout the 1990s, and for much of the following decade.

Table 5.3 shows how kibbutz members have perceived the economic condition of their kibbutzim in selected years between 1989 and 2011. In

TABLE 5.3.
Members' Perceptions of the Economic
Condition of Their Kibbutz, 1989–2011

		Economic condition of the kibbutz (%)		
Year	Population surveyed	Not good	Average	Good
2011	All kibbutzim	12	33	55
2009	All kibbutzim	21	38	41
2007	All kibbutzim	22	33	45
2005	All kibbutzim	28	34	38
2004	All kibbutzim	31	35	34
2002	All kibbutzim	43	30	27
2001	Takam kibbutzim	39	33	28
	Artzi kibbutzum	35	40	25
2000	Takam kibbutzim	41	29	30
	Artzi kibbutzim	37	29	34
1998	Takam kibbutzim	41	29	30
	Artzi kibbutzim	34	37	29
1989	Takam kibbutzim	43	38	19
	Artzi kibbutzim	49	35	16

Source: Palgi and Orchan 2011, 11.

1989, well over 40 percent of kibbutz members in both kibbutz federations saw the economic condition of their kibbutz as "not good," and fewer than 20 percent in each federation described the economic condition of their kibbutz as "good." In the years 1998, 2000, and 2001, kibbutz members gave slightly more optimistic assessments, but in 2002, their perceptions were almost as pessimistic as in 1989, with 43 percent of all kibbutz members seeing the economic condition of their kibbutz as "not good." Only in recent years is there evidence of steady improvement in the economic condition of the kibbutzim. By 2011, the proportion of kibbutz members describing the economic condition of their kibbutz as "not good" had fallen to 12 percent, with 55 percent of kibbutz members seeing the economic condition of their kibbutz as "good."

Although the economic condition of the kibbutzim showed signs of improvement in the first decade of the new century, the demographic condition of the kibbutzim remained problematic in many ways. As previously noted, the number of kibbutz members continued to decline, and the number of children living on kibbutzim was falling even faster. As recently as 2006, the total kibbutz population, at 122,747, remained below what it had been in 1990 (125,100). Only in the years since 2008 has the total population of the kibbutzim climbed back above its 1990 level (see tables 1.1 and 5.2).

From Inertia to Institutional Entrepreneurship

Like other organizations, the kibbutzim possess varying amounts of organizational inertia. That the kibbutzim were once famous for their stability indicates that they at one time possessed high levels of organizational inertia. After years of resisting change, the kibbutzim have lost their organizational inertia, and show little sign of regaining it.

In 1990, the kibbutzim committed themselves to introduce reforms, but conservative voices in the federations and within each kibbutz warned that these changes should not go too far. Decisions about which reforms to adopt in each kibbutz were often hotly contested. In the early 1990s, only modest innovations gained acceptance; even they spread with great hesitation and uncertainty. Changes that were under discussion in one year were, in the next year, as likely to have been dropped from consideration, or to remain under discussion, as they were to have been accepted. Even after the members of a kibbutz voted in favor of a change, changes were often abandoned during the process of implementation or after they had been adopted.

Once a substantial number of reforms began to spread, it became possible to identify which organizations had more inertia and which had less, simply by counting the number of changes the organization had previously made. This count can be interpreted as either a measure of the extent to which an organization is generally open to change, or as a measure of the impact of change on the organization that adopts it. As we saw in both chapter 3 and chapter 4, this measure turned out to be a very important predictor of whether a kibbutz would introduce additional modest reforms and more radical transformation. The more inertia a kibbutz has shown in the past, the more likely it is to remain unchanged in the future; the more reforms a kibbutz has introduced in the past, the more likely it becomes to introduce additional reforms and transformations.

In the first years of the new century, the period of modest reform gave rise to a period of more radical transformation. By the end of the decade, three-quarters of all nonreligious kibbutzim had become kibbutzim of a new type. Thus the kibbutzim have lost their organizational inertia, and are searching for ways to get their stability back.

During both the period of reform and that of the later transformation, kibbutz members made decisions in the context of high levels of uncertainty. They introduced individual reforms, without knowledge of the larger changes to which these ostensibly modest changes would eventually lead. Most kibbutzim committed themselves to pay differential salaries, at a time when it was not clear whether kibbutzim that adopted this practice would be allowed to continue to call themselves kibbutzim.

To cope with these high levels of uncertainty, both individual kibbutzim and the kibbutz population as a whole accumulated growing quantities of experience and expertise. Within each kibbutz, both phases began with the appointment of special committees to facilitate change in that kibbutz. Managers with experience of change in one kibbutz later serve as consultants in others. For kibbutzim whose members were confused or deeply divided, figures like Israel Tsufim and Israel Oz served as institutional entrepreneurs, articulating a vision of the future of the kibbutz that incorporated traditional kibbutz values.

Mechanisms of Isomorphism

In *Institutions and Organizations*, Scott (2008) divides the institutional processes affecting organizations into three major kinds: regulative, normative, and cognitive. In their classic essay on the causes of homogeneity among organizations in the same field, Paul DiMaggio and Walter W. Powell (1983) similarly identify three "mechanisms of institutional isomorphism." *Coercive* isomorphism "results from both formal and informal pressures exerted on organizations by other organizations on which they are dependent" (DiMaggio and Powell 1983, 150). It is best illustrated by the role of the state in authorizing or requiring various forms of organization and ways of doing business. *Mimetic* isomorphism results from the tendency of organizations to model themselves on other organizations in the face of uncertainty or ambiguity. *Normative* pressures promoting similarity in organizations "stem primarily from professionalization." DiMaggio and Powell note in particular that "professional and trade associations" serve as important vehicles "for the definition and promulgation of normative rules about organizational and professional behavior" (1983, 152).

If we apply this terminology to the recent changes in the kibbutzim, mimetic isomorphism has clearly played a prominent role during this period. At every stage of these changes, the kibbutzim have been strongly influenced by the examples set by other kibbutzim, adopting changes that substantial numbers of other kibbutzim have introduced, and avoiding changes that other kibbutzim also have avoided. This tendency of the kibbutzim to imitate and learn from one another has been the most persistent influence seen throughout these analyses.

Although, among the kibbutzim, late adopters of innovations have been imitating early adopters, both sets of kibbutzim have also been imitating examples set by market-oriented, profit-seeking businesses of all types. As table 4.2 demonstrates, the adoption of differential salaries by kibbutzim has brought with it not only a new set of practices, but also a new set of organizational titles and a completely new institutional logic. Although the architects of the renewed kibbutz had no common theory, they shared an agenda of replacing kibbutz approaches to problems and decisions with more conventional business solutions and practices. Moreover, if managerial positions in kibbutzim were to be made open to nonmembers, they needed to be described in terms that would be meaningful and attractive to managers arriving from outside.

Compared to this strong influence of mimetic isomorphism, normative influences have apparently been far less important. Since DiMaggio and Powell (1983) associate normative isomorphism with the influence of professional bodies, we have looked for evidence of these effects by comparing kibbutzim associated with the Artzi Federation to those associated with Takam. Although we have, at several phases of these analyses, documented statistically significant differences between Artzi and Takam kibbutzim, we have found that, in the end, neither federation succeeded in preventing a majority of its members from paying differential salaries to members, despite threats from both federations to expel any kibbutzim that did.

During much of this transformation, Israeli regulatory authorities have come across as even more impotent than the federations. Despite threats from the Registrar of Cooperatives, between 1995 and 2005 a majority of the kibbutzim transformed their structures in ways that were not permitted by Israel's Law of Cooperatives, and these kibbutzim suffered no penalty for doing so. When the state did belatedly become involved, its action was primarily to give its blessing to changes that had already occurred.

The Registrar of Cooperatives has played only a modest role in this transformation, but other agencies of the Israeli government have been involved in important ways. In 1985, it was a sudden shift in the economic policies of the Israeli government that led to the bankruptcy of the kibbutzim. A few years later, in its role as the principal creditor to the kibbutzim, the state took the lead in forcing the kibbutzim to commit themselves to reforms.

Although the Israeli government was slow to become involved in clarifying the identity of kibbutzim that paid differential salaries, when it did, its intervention was decisive. The Public Committee on the Kibbutzim that was formed in 2002 included respected figures from academia, the kibbutz movement, and the Israeli government. When the Public Committee's report was issued in 2003, its recommendations were quickly accepted both by the kibbutz movement and by the government. By defining kibbutzim that paid kibbutzim differential salaries as kibbutzim of a new type, but still kibbutzim, Eliezer Ben-Rafael's committee played an important role in preserving the unity of the kibbutz movement during this period of transformative change. In labeling the new type of kibbutzim renewed kibbutzim, rather than differential kibbutzim, the Public Committee appears to have been looking for a way to express encouragement, rather than just acceptance, for the new form.

Since the recommendations of the Public Committee became law in 2005, Israel's Registrar of Cooperatives is no longer a passive observer of the transformation of traditional kibbutzim into kibbutzim that pay differential salaries. Now the Registrar of Cooperatives has a written definition laying out what a renewed kibbutz can and cannot do, and has begun to enforce these standards when kibbutzim ask to change their designation from collective kibbutz to renewed.

Finally, when proposed changes involve not only compensation, but also the ownership of the kibbutz, a vote by the members in favor of the change is just the first step in a long process. The next step is often the courts. Plans to distribute shares of stock or ownership of housing among kibbutz members may be challenged by members or children of members who feel unfairly disadvantaged by the plan. Because kibbutz land is agricultural land, proposals to rezone some of it as residential housing require the approval of Israel's Land Authority. Because the land that most kibbutzim are located is owned by the Jewish National Fund, various groups have asserted both in the courts and in the government that the kibbutzim should not be allowed to profit by converting publicly owned land into privately owned housing.

Varieties of Kibbutzim

By 2011, 188 of Israel's 248 nonreligious kibbutzim had abandoned their traditional practice of allocating resources on the basis of need, and had begun paying differential salaries. Of the remaining nonreligious kibbutzim, 7 had mixed systems of compensation, and 53 kibbutzim continued to base compensation solely on need.

In this section, we provide a few comments about current trends affecting each of the principal alternatives to, and variations upon, the renewed kibbutz. In addition to considering the collective and mixed kibbutzim, we also incorporate the latest information available about the religious kibbutzim and about such new varieties of kibbutzim as urban kibbutzim and ecological kibbutzim.

Collective Kibbutzim

In chapter 4, we have already noted that kibbutzim facing greater economic difficulty were more likely than others to transform themselves into kibbutzim of the mixed or renewed types. Because these transformations did little in the short term to improve the economic performance of the kibbutzim making them (Russell, Hanneman, and Getz 2010), these differences in economic condition have tended to persist. In 2011, 75 percent of members of collective kibbutzim perceived the economic condition of their kibbutz as "good," whereas only 48 percent of members of kibbutzim paying differential salaries described the economic condition of their kibbutz so favorably. The proportions of members describing the economic condition of their kibbutz as "bad," in contrast, was 15 percent in kibbutzim with differential salaries, and only 6 percent in collective kibbutzim.

Kibbutz members are well aware of this difference in the economic condition of collective and renewed kibbutzim. Many comment on the irony in seeing the kibbutz turn into a system of socialism for the rich and capitalism for the poor. Some wryly joke that kibbutz members still like socialism, but now they are forced to ask themselves how much socialism can they afford.

Although members of collective kibbutzim are insulated by affluence and often by remote geographic locations from the more urgent pressures for change, they take special interest in some kinds of reforms. Some of the collective kibbutzim belong to an organization that provides advice about reforms suitable for collective kibbutzim. The most influential advisor to the collective kibbutzim is Elisha Shapira, who served previously as head of the Artzi federation. As an alternative to paying market-based salaries, members of this group recommend, there should be differential budgetary allocations based on seniority, with seniority defined as the number of years a person has been a member of the kibbutz.

Members of collective kibbutzim share some aspirations with members of other kibbutzim that may lead them eventually to follow the example of these others into becoming renewed kibbutzim. Most members of collective kibbutzim now join members of renewed kibbutzim in believing that distributing kibbutz property to individual members would be more helpful than harmful to their kibbutz (Palgi and Orchan 2011, 70). When kibbutz members were polled in 2007 and 2009 about specific ways to transfer kibbutz property to individuals, such as distributing shares in kibbutz enterprises to members on the basis of seniority (Palgi and Orchan 2009, 50) and allowing members to leave shares to their children (Palgi and Orchan 2007, 57), overwhelming majorities of the members in collective, mixed, and differential kibbutzim expressed support for both changes.

Kibbutzim of the Mixed Type

In the highly important formative years of the late 1990s, kibbutzim with mixed compensation systems outnumbered kibbutzim with safety-net budgets. For many years thereafter, pollsters and statisticians continued to classify the mixed type as a major alternative to the need-based and fully differential models. By 2011, however, the number of kibbutzim conforming to the mixed model had shrunk to seven. Because this category is now too small to provide a reliable basis for sampling, the Institute for Research of the Kibbutz no longer includes the mixed kibbutzim as a type in its biennial surveys of kibbutz members.

Although kibbutzim with mixed compensation are numerically of little importance today, the mixed type has earned a prominent place in the history of the transition from need-based to market-based compensation on the kibbutzim. At a time when it was ideologically and politically difficult for an individual kibbutz to embrace differential compensation, the mixed kibbutz served as a convenient "transitional identity" (Clark et al. 2010), to help ease the passage from one type to another. This unstable mix of two contradictory institutional logics was especially attractive to kibbutzim that had been losing members and were trying to minimize the further loss of members that might result from an irrevocable commitment to a completely new organizational identity (Russell, Hanneman, and Getz 2010).

Religious Kibbutzim

Even though kibbutzim of the mixed type have proved to be a transitory phenomenon, the religious kibbutz endures as the most important alternative to the better-known varieties of kibbutzim. There are sixteen religious kibbutzim, of which nine were established between 1937 and 1952 and the other seven between 1966 and 1982. Whereas the secular kibbutzim derive many of their collective ideals from socialism, the religious kibbutzim root their communalism in the Torah (Fishman 1992; Katz 1999).

The religious kibbutzim are generally more prosperous than the secular kibbutzim. They did not suffer as much as other kibbutzim from the economic crisis of the 1980s, and did not participate in the 1989 agreement among the government, the banks, and the kibbutzim that committed the kibbutzim to introduce reforms.

By 2012, three of the nine older religious kibbutzim had transformed themselves into renewed kibbutzim, and so had four of the seven younger ones. As in Michael Hannan and John Freeman's (1984) theory of organizational inertia, it was the younger kibbutzim that were first to make this change.

Table 5.2 shows that the population of the religious kibbutzim declined from 6,000 in 1998 to 5,856 in the year 2000, but then grew to 10,888 in 2010, an increase of 85.6 percent. Spread over sixteen kibbutzim, this total represents an average population of 681 per kibbutz, substantially larger than the secular kibbutzim.

Urban Kibbutzim and Communal Groups
The religious kibbutzim trace their roots to the 1930s and 1940s, but a more recent development associated with the kibbutz movement has been the emergence of kibbutzim and communes within Israel's cities. Members of these urban kibbutzim and communes spend their days working as teachers or social workers or in other helping professions, but gather after work to pool their incomes and live together in communal households.

The kibbutz movement had tried to establish such urban kibbutzim several times in the past, but it was not until 1979 that it achieved its first success. As Yuval Dror reported in 2011, "The first urban kibbutz was established in Jerusalem in 1979. Today there are four urban kibbutzim in Israel: Reshit (Kiryat-Menachem, Jerusalem, founded in 1979); Tamuz (Beit Shemesh, founded in 1987); Migvan (Sderot, founded in 1987); Beit Israel (Gilo, Jerusalem, founded in 1992). Each numbers dozens of members, living on various levels communally, while additional families and single people participate in their educational and other community work without becoming members of the kibbutz" (Dror 2011, 316).

When Ben-Rafael's Public Committee issued its report on the legal definition of the kibbutzim, it recommended that the law be expanded to give recognition not only to the renewed kibbutz, but also to the urban kibbutz, defined as "a community living a communal life in a town or a city" (Dror 2011, 318). In keeping with this recommendation, Israeli law now identifies three types of kibbutzim: the collective kibbutz, the renewed kibbutz, and the urban kibbutz.

The urban kibbutzim were initially established with the cooperation and encouragement of the kibbutz movement, and they were founded by young adults most of whom had grown up on kibbutzim. Since the 1980s, large numbers of small and amorphous communes have emerged in cities all over Israel, communes that have no ties of any kind to the kibbutz movement. Many of these urban communes have been created by graduates of Zionist youth movements in Israel and the Diaspora. In past decades, these youth movements and associated institutions, such as the army's Nahal, prepared young people for futures in kibbutzim. Now, members of these movements perceive the kibbutzim as having abandoned their communal values. These movements now encourage their graduates to create new communal institutions with a new mission. Whereas the original kibbutzim aimed to settle Jews on the land of Israel, members of the urban kibbutzim and communes seek to deliver educational and social services to underprivileged populations in Israel's cities.

The growing disaffection between the kibbutz movement and the youth movements had not only an ideological but also a structural dimension. Until the 1980s, the kibbutz federations recognized the youth movements as important sources of new members for the kibbutzim, and they sent emissaries and material support to these movements in return. When the crisis of the 1980s caused the kibbutzim to run short of both money and ideological commitment, the support the federations gave to the youth movements sharply declined. In the words of Dror (2011), "The changing kibbutz, plagued by crises, ceased to attract urban youth in search of worthy goals, leading to a sharp drop in the number of youth movement members, [of] graduates that served as 'Nahal' soldiers (branch of the Israeli army) that aimed to join the kibbutzim, and above all of those choosing kibbutz life. This reduced still further the number of kibbutz members active in the youth movements and the financial support they received, since the kibbutzim realized that they did not benefit from this expenditure and no longer felt committed to assist them, creating a vicious circle" (Dror 2011, 319).

James Horrox estimated in 2009, "At the time of writing, there are upwards of 1,500 people living communally across Israel, entirely unconnected to the kibbutz movement. . . . Approximately three-quarters of these are members of the Tnuat Bogrim or graduate movement groups of the youth movement Noar ve'Lomed (Working and Student Youth Movement), otherwise known by its acronym NOAL" (2009, 104). Other youth movements encouraging their graduates to live together in urban communes are Mahanot Haolim and Hashomer Hatzair in Israel and Habonim Dror in the Diaspora. Horrox suggests that Israel's contemporary urban kibbutzim and communal groups now benefit from the youthful idealism that in previous generations fed the development of the classic kibbutzim. In his words, "As kibbutz life was supposedly the ultimate fulfillment of their ideology, the kibbutz's abandonment of its original values left graduates of the youth movement without a means of achieving *hagshama* (self-realisation) or any structure for bringing about change in Israeli society. Many NOAL graduates began to look for alternatives. In the creation of new, more intimate settlements, they saw a way of achieving hagshama by practising the youth movement's ideology and values in their daily lives" (Horrox 2009, 104).

Even though members of the urban communal groups are critical of the contemporary kibbutzim, many groups model themselves after the kvutzot from which the kibbutz movement later emerged. Horrox notes, "The fact that these groups choose to describe themselves as 'kvutzot' rather than kibbutzim is itself a deliberate and conscious alignment with the intimacy of the small anarchistic settlements of the early years" (Horrox 2009, 105).

Ecological Kibbutzim

Among kibbutzim that have historically been part of the kibbutz movement, the one set of organizations with an élan that in some cases rivals that of the urban kibbutzim and communes is the so-called ecological kibbutzim (Livni 2011). In recent years, growing numbers of kibbutzim have begun to identify themselves as ecological kibbutzim. In 2007, for example, a sign at the front gate of Kibbutz Sassa in northern Israel declared it to be "A Renewed Kibbutz with an Ecological Vision." Kibbutz Lotan in the Negev desert adopted a philosophy of "eco-Zionism" years earlier. It is the only kibbutz to become part of the Global Ecological Network, and has made the goal of living in harmony with its desert environment a part of its vision statement. Kibbutz Nir Oz, also in the Negev, committed itself to water-wise agriculture as early as 1962; it harvests rainwater to use in irrigation, desalinates sea water, and has identified or developed more than nine hundred species of plants that require no irrigation. Other kibbutzim that have taken up the cause of environmental protection and/or organic gardening include Kibbutz Ketura, Kibbutz Neot Smadar, and Kibbutz Sde Eliyahu (Livni 2011).

Although members of ecological kibbutzim often speak with great pride about events and achievements on their own kibbutz, the ecological kibbutzim have not yet developed a common identity or clearly articulated ideology. To date, their efforts have remained uncoordinated, leaving other kibbutzim to increase their consciousness of the environment one kibbutz at a time.

Types of Kibbutzim

Now, as in their earliest decades, the kibbutzim clearly come in more than one type. In the first half of the twentieth century, the most important competing alternatives were the kvutzah and the kibbutz. In the early twenty-first century, the principal alternatives are the collective kibbutz and the renewed kibbutz, with small numbers of additional kibbutzim either opting for the mixed model or adhering to more sharply focused organizational identities such of those of the religious, urban, and ecological kibbutzim.

Although today, as in the past, the kibbutzim come in several varieties, none of the current alternatives seriously challenges the ascendancy of the renewed kibbutz. The renewed kibbutz is now clearly the dominant organizational form among the kibbutzim.

Common Trends

In the preceding section, we have surveyed the extent of diversity found among contemporary kibbutzim. This section complements that discussion by identifying themes and concerns that most or all contemporary kibbutzim have in common. These include: efforts to privatize the ownership of kibbutz assets, the importance attached to demographic growth, the widespread municipalization of kibbutz governance, and the changing relationship between the kibbutzim and Israeli society.

Privatizing the Ownership of Kibbutz Assets

The report of Ben-Rafael's Public Committee identified three changes, any one of which transformed a collective kibbutz into a renewed kibbutz: differential salaries, transfer of ownership of kibbutz housing to individual members, and transfer of ownership of other kibbutz assets to individual members. Of these three changes, unequal pay was the first to be introduced and therefore bears primary responsibility for transforming more than three-quarters of all nonreligious kibbutzim into renewed kibbutzim in the years 1995 through 2011.

As the issue of compensation has been decided on most kibbutzim, attention has shifted to changes in the ownership of housing and other assets. Kibbutz members have differing opinions about the desirability of particular forms of compensation, but majorities of members in both renewed and collective kibbutzim in 2011 agreed that distributing kibbutz property to individual members would be more helpful than harmful (Palgi and Orchan 2011, 70). Many kibbutz members favor distributing shares in profit-making ventures on the basis of seniority, so that a member who has worked in the kibbutz for thirty or forty years will receive more shares than a member who has worked in the kibbutz for only a few years. In kibbutzim that have distributed shares to date, 30 percent to 50 percent of shares have been distributed equally and 50 percent to 70 percent according to seniority. Until such questions have been decided, veteran kibbutz members have hesitated to admit new members.

The aging of the kibbutz membership adds to pressure to transfer collective assets to individuals, because aging members want to secure their claims on the capital of the kibbutz. In past generations, when kibbutz parents dreamed that their children would someday join them on the kibbutz, the continuity of the kibbutz was their legacy to their children. Now, their children live in cities. When the children try to buy homes, they find themselves in competition with bidders whose parents help them pay the cost. Kibbutz members now live in homes to which they have added rooms or made other major improvements at their own expense. Increasingly kibbutz members are looking for ways to recoup some of the gains from their past investments in kibbutz businesses and kibbutz housing, and to transfer these assets to their children.

In 1996, the Israeli Land Authority authorized allocation of land to individual members of *moshavim* and kibbutzim under certain conditions. In the year 2000, some kibbutzim initiated transfers of housing to individual members in accordance with this policy. Only four or five kibbutzim had completed these transfers, however, before a 2002 Supreme Court decision challenged the right of the kibbutzim to sell or to give away any land belonging to the Jewish National Fund (JNF), and brought all such transfers to a halt. This decision, which became known as the "distributive justice" decision, applied to both the kibbutzim and the moshavim, and, as have noted, questioned the right of either to profit by selling land belonging to the JNF. For the past decade, the Israel Land Authority and the kibbutz federation have failed to agree on a legal way to complete these property transfers. The kibbutz federation now advises its members to allocate homes to members by means of so-called internal allocation. Such internal allocation would be accomplished by means of a contract between the kibbutz and the individual member allocating the land and any house on it to the individual member.

Uncertainty about what rights of home ownership will or will not be included with kibbutz membership is one of the main factors retarding the admission of new members to kibbutzim in recent years. Some kibbutzim are now experimenting with new classes of membership that confer the right to build or buy a house on the kibbutz, or that make the member a homeowner but do not include participation in the collective economy of the kibbutz.

Although these legal and political complications have been a source of tremendous frustration for kibbutz members impatient for change, they illustrate once again the extent to which the identity of the kibbutzim has been institutionalized in Israeli society. This identity has not only been codified in Israeli law; it is also regularly readjudicated in decisions handed down by the Land Authority and by the courts. Because the kibbutzim are located on land owned by the JNF, the Israeli government and Israeli courts claim jurisdiction over all changes in the ownership of land and housing on the kibbutzim.

Importance Attached to Demographic Growth

Although the perceived economic difficulties of the kibbutzim have showed signs of subsiding in recent years, the demographic problems of the kibbutzim have been both more persistent and more widely spread.

The proportion of members who saw it as urgent for their kibbutz to deal with demographic growth ranged in 2009 from 64 percent on the collective kibbutzim to 74 percent on the mixed type of kibbutz and 78 percent on kibbutzim with differential salaries (Palgi and Orchan 2009). As with economic problems, the perceived urgency of demographic difficulties is higher on the differential and mixed types of kibbutzim than on the collective kibbutzim, but, with demographic problems, overwhelming majorities of members on all three types of kibbutzim see the issues as critical.

If we compare the early history of the kibbutzim to that of recent decades, one commonality stands out. Both in the early twentieth century and again at the start of the twenty-first, the kibbutzim adopted structures to enhance their appeal to the ideals and aspirations of potential members. The collective kibbutz was a great way to tap the idealism of Jewish immigrants to Palestine in the pre-state period, but it has little appeal for contemporary Israelis; in hope of attracting a new generation of Israelis, the kibbutzim have transformed themselves into kibbutzim of a new type.

The economic and demographic health of all kibbutzim has become increasingly dependent on their ability to attract nonmembers to live among them as neighbors, to patronize their services, and to take jobs in their businesses. In recent years, the kibbutzim have shifted the focus of their recruitment efforts from preparing people to become members to encouraging people to live on a kibbutz, send their children to kibbutz schools, and patronize other kibbutz services. The stated goal now is "demographic growth," and persuading nonmembers to live in the neighborhoods being built for them on many kibbutzim is now widely seen as offering the kibbutzim their best chance of achieving this end. As places to live, the kibbutzim offer many attractions, from park-like landscaping to secure perimeters. Thanks to their schools and clinics, they are perceived as especially good places to raise children or to grow old.

Although kibbutz members and nonmembers now frequently encounter one another as shoppers in kibbutz convenience stores, or as students and parents associated with kibbutz schools, they meet as strangers, not as acquaintances, and their interests often conflict on many issues. One common problem, for example, is that developers who build new neighborhoods on kibbutzim often fail to complete the projects, and the kibbutzim on which these developments are located are slow to accept responsibility for finishing the work (Greenberg 2011). The need to overcome the gulf between members and permanent residents is one of the most important reasons why many kibbutzim are trying to create new categories of membership, and are also trying to create new forms of governance for their communities, forms that include representation both for kibbutz members, who participate in the collective economy, and for other permanent residents.

Municipalization of the Kibbutzim

As the proportion of kibbutz residents who are nonmembers continues to grow, many kibbutz communities have begun to transform themselves into entities that function more like municipalities, and in which both kibbutz members and nonmembers have rights of representation. Israeli law provides that home owners who are not members of kibbutzim must be given rights of representation in the governance of local services such as education, water, power, and sanitation. In many kibbutzim, the kibbutz secretariat that formerly ran the entire kibbutz as one unit is now divided into two separate committees: a kibbutz secretariat that is responsible for kibbutz communal assets and kibbutz members, and a municipal secretariat that takes care of local services and includes all residents, both kibbutz members and nonmember home owners.

To accommodate such changes, one possibility being considered on some kibbutzim is to transform the kibbutz into a moshav. Another alternative is to become a *yishuv kehilati* (a term that can be translated as "community settlement" or as "incorporated community"). Like a municipality, a yishuv kehilati provides members with basic local services such as refuse collection, water, and sanitation.

In 2007, Michal Palgi and Elliette Orchan asked kibbutz members to identify which of the following types of life would suit them best: collective kibbutz, renewed kibbutz, moshav, yishuv kehilati, or city. The researchers found that in no type of kibbutz did a majority of the members prefer to live in the type of kibbutz that they in fact resided in. The type of kibbutz that was most popular among its own members was the collective kibbutz; there, 44 percent of the members preferred to live in a kibbutz of that type. (Even in the collective kibbutz, however, 56 percent of the members would have preferred to live in a community of a different type.) In the mixed kibbutzim, members' sympathies were divided about equally among the collective kibbutz (29 percent), the renewed kibbutz (35 percent), and a yishuv kehilati (27 percent). In the kibbutzim with systems of differential salaries, the proportion of members who would prefer to live in yishuv kehilati (35 percent) exceeded the proportion preferring a renewed kibbutz such as the one on which they currently lived (34 percent).

The Kibbutzim and Israeli Society

In their earliest decades, the kibbutzim sought to set an example for their society that would someday help to transform that society and the world as a whole. The model kibbutz bylaws that the federations disseminated in the 1970s included a declaration that the kibbutz "aims to establish in Israel a socialist society, based on economic and social equality" (Yassour 1977, 315). In recent years, the kibbutzim have sought less to change Israeli society than to fit into it.

As early as the 1970s, the sociologist Eric Cohen was sensitive to the threats that growing differentiation and individuation posed to the historic identity and sense of mission of the kibbutzim. Indeed, he ended his essay "The Structural Transformation of the Kibbutz" by commenting:

> We find that the kibbutz has become more vigorous than ever before through the processes of industrialization, modernization, and urbanization. Nowadays, it forms an integral and important sector of Israeli society. However, these developments also changed profoundly the nature of the institutional arrangements and social relations in the kibbutz and thus put into question its ability to preserve its unique social characteristics. The large and mature kibbutz may easily become just another form of modern urban life, distinguishable from other such forms merely by some peculiar arrangements and institutions, but losing most of its historically distinguishing characteristics as a revolutionary communal and corporate entity. (1983, 109–110)

The traditional kibbutz sought to meet all the needs of its members. Members ate in the kibbutz dining hall, sent their children to the kibbutz educational system, and attended kibbutz-sponsored cultural events. This had the effect of isolating the daily life of the kibbutz from the life of surrounding geographical areas. Today, kibbutzim in remote locations such as the Negev are among those most likely to remain loyal to the collective form. Whereas the collective kibbutz is now best preserved among kibbutzim that have minimal contact with the surrounding society, the renewed kibbutz explicitly embraces it. This new strategy of appealing to nonmembers has the potential to provide the kibbutzim with the resources they need to survive, but at the cost of further eroding their unique identities. The kibbutzim may in time become so thoroughly integrated into the rest of Israeli society, that they become indistinguishable from it.

The Renewal of the Kibbutzim

If we compare the final chapter of this work to the first one, a few persistent themes can be discerned, despite the many differences in terminology. One is the theme of change. The kibbutzim are changing now, but they have changed before in many ways at many times in their history. The industrialization of the kibbutzim, the shift from collective to individual consumption, and the shift from communal to household-based childrearing, for example, are all changes that began long before the changes described in this work and that may have been of comparable or even greater significance.

Another common theme linking early and later episodes in the history of the kibbutzim is that, in the words of Yitzhak Tabenkin, "the kibbutz came before its idea. It had no preplan" (Kellerman 1993, 50). At multiple turning points in kibbutz history, members invented new forms of organization in acts of improvisation and institutional entrepreneurship, and let others decide later what to say about them. We saw this first in the formation of the first kvutzah at Degania in 1910, which later came to be acknowledged as the birth date of the kibbutzim. In the 1970s and 1980s, individual kibbutz members and individual kibbutzim shifted from communal childrearing to family-based sleeping household by household and kibbutz by kibbutz, until eventually the leaders of the federations were forced to accept a change that they had been unable to prevent. Between 1995 and 2005, similarly, a more than half of Israel's 248 nonreligious kibbutzim began paying differential salaries to their members, even though Israel's Law of Cooperatives did not permit kibbutzim to make such a change at the time.

By the year 2011, more than three-quarters of Israel's nonreligious kibbutzim had voted to adopt differential payment systems. The kibbutzim that have voted to renew their identities by making this change were committing themselves not so much to a clear outcome, as to a process of transformation. Members of all three types of kibbutzim want their kibbutzim to make additional changes in the ownership of housing and other assets. Kibbutz members want to own their own homes, and they want to offer that same opportunity to nonmembers. Where these changes will lead the kibbutzim remains hard to predict. It is also hard to predict whether all kibbutzim will make these changes in ways that keep them part of the same population of organizations.

We began this chapter by showing that academic, governmental, and kibbutz movement sources all agree that a kibbutz that pays individual market-based salaries to its members is a different kind of organization from a kibbutz that shares resources on the basis of need. The three-quarters or more of kibbutzim that have introduced this innovation were not merely reformed by this change; they were transformed by it.

Most kibbutzim are still entitled to be described as democratic, cooperative, and communal organizations, in at least some senses of these terms, but such labels become less applicable to kibbutzim with each passing day. Increasingly, it is the general properties of kibbutzim *as organizations* that have the greatest influence on the way they change. These general characteristics shared with other organizations include the need for resources, their relative inertia or experience with change, and their readiness to learn from examples set by other organizations of the same sort.

The kibbutzim have lost their inertia and show little sign of regaining it. Economic and demographic problems persist on many. Additional changes, in such areas as the ownership of housing and of economic ventures, are widely discussed. Some kibbutzim are exploring the possibility of transforming themselves into organizations of completely different types, such as a moshav or a yishuv kehilati.

Officially, the introduction of differential salaries or private ownership on a kibbutz signifies not the end of the kibbutz, but its renewal. Whether the individual kibbutzim and the kibbutz movement as a whole will in fact be renewed by this transformation remains to be seen. This uncertainty about the direction in which the kibbutzim are headed is reflected in the lack of consensus about how kibbutzim with differential salaries or private ownership can best be described. As we noted, Israeli sources label such kibbutzim differential kibbutzim, safety-net kibbutzim, or privatized kibbutzim, while few voices outside of government or academia refer to them as renewed or "renewing" kibbutzim. We have titled this work *The Renewal of the Kibbutz*, not *The Privatization of the Kibbutz*, because we share the expectation that the recent changes in the kibbutzim do not signify the end of these unique organizations, but merely constitute a new chapter in their history.

While this book is clearly a story of renewal, it is a story that has a shift in emphasis. We began chapter 4 watching individual kibbutzim transform their identities, through acts of institutional entrepreneurship that originally took place one organization at a time. By the end of that chapter, we saw the safety-net budget become the most popular form of compensation among the kibbutzim, as it spread by imitation from one kibbutz to the other. In chapter 5, our attention shifted to the kibbutz federations and the Israeli government, watching them adjudicate the fit between this innovation and existing legal definitions of a kibbutz. We saw that, on the advice of Ben-Rafael's Public Committee, these bodies agreed to label a kibbutz that paid differential salaries a kibbutz that had been renewed. In light of these decisions, we came to realize, it is no longer solely individual organizations that have been renewed by these changes, but our entire conception of what a kibbutz is. The fundamental identity of the kibbutz has been radically altered, both in law and in fact.

In this book, we have followed the example set by Manor (2004) in translating the term *kibbutz mithadesh* as "renewed kibbutz." A more literal translation of the Hebrew word *mithadesh*, however, would render this term as "renewing kibbutz" (Ben-Rafael and Topel 2011). It is worthwhile to note this distinction here, because it means that when kibbutz members voted to adopt the identity of a kibbutz mithadesh, they viewed this act not as the end of a process of transformation, but as a beginning.

APPENDIX: DATA SOURCES AND STATISTICAL ANALYTICS

In several chapters we present quantitative portraits of the process and consequences of innovation in the kibbutzim. The purpose of this appendix is to provide documentation of the samples and data used in our statistical analyses, and to explain the approaches we used in analyzing the data.

Surveys of Changes in Kibbutzim

Chapters 2 through 4 make use of data derived from surveys of changes in kibbutzim conducted annually by the Institute for Research of the Kibbutz at the University of Haifa from 1990 through 2001. We begin this appendix by providing additional information about this survey.

Survey Content and Responses

The annual surveys carried out by the Institute for Research of the Kibbutz were conducted in association with the two major kibbutz federations, and their aim was to include all of the reforms that were being introduced or being discussed on one or more kibbutzim at the time of a given survey. The primary sources of this information were publications of the kibbutz movements. Until their recent merger, both Takam and the Artzi federation produced weekly newsletters. Now the combined kibbutz movement puts out a single newsletter; the articles for these newsletters are written by professional journalists, not office holders, and this helps to make them informative and up to date.

Another important source of changes included in annual surveys was the reports of change committees. Because the kibbutzim promised the government in 1989 that they would introduce reforms, many set up change committees in the early 1990s. It was the charge of these committees to collect ideas for change from other kibbutzim, and then to use these as a basis for making proposals for changing their own kibbutz. Reports of change committees soon began to be circulated from one kibbutz to another.

Reports of change committees were useful primarily at the beginning of the 1990s, as were the proposals of reformers like Yehuda Harel and Dudik Rutenberg. In later years, the Institute's researchers became increasingly dependent on what they were hearing other kibbutz members talk about.

To survey the kibbutzim about a change, the change had to have a name. In 1990 the terms used to describe many changes varied from kibbutz to kibbutz. Many terms were ambiguous, ambivalent, or politically charged. For example, having members pay for electricity was called privatization of electricity in one kibbutz and not in another. Researchers at the Institute worded items for the questionnaire in the most general terms possible, but added a supplementary instruction to the kibbutz secretaries who were filling out the forms, noting that some changes might be known by different names.

In years after 1990, researchers conducting the survey continued to monitor changes being proposed in kibbutz journals, and asked their colleagues at the Institute if they knew of other changes that needed to be added. For a change to be added to the survey, at least one kibbutz had to be already using it, or at least one kibbutz journal had to be proposing it. The intention was to keep a new proposal on the questionnaire for one or two years, and then to drop it if no one took up the idea.

To make room for new proposals, a number of questions were deleted from the survey, over the years. Accepting children of nonmembers in kibbutz daycare facilities and schools was dropped from the survey in 1996, because it appeared to have been decided by consensus. By that time, 89.7 percent of kibbutzim were reporting that they were doing this, and the few kibbutzim not doing it began to add excuses for their exceptional behavior, such as that they had no Jewish neighbors. The "comprehensive budget," similarly, had become widely accepted (74.7 percent) by the time it was dropped from the survey in 1996, the year in which it began to be displaced by the new "safety-net budget." "Members paying for electricity," however, was retained in all years of the survey, for use in identifying conservative kibbutzim that were unusually immune to change.

Some items were dropped from the survey because of validity problems. One set of such problems arose when questions tried to differentiate between two or more similar-sounding reforms. For example, kibbutzim had created boards of directors for factories, for farms, for all kibbutz productive activities, and for the kibbutz as a whole; in 1999, the survey asked about many of these different types of board. Some respondents seem to have been confused by the overly detailed specification of types of boards, causing the question about a board of directors "for the community" to be dropped after 1999.

Similarly, kibbutzim experimented in the 1990s with ways to pay their members extra money for extra work. In some years, the survey included specific questions about whether such extra payments could be earned on the basis of working extra days, working extra hours, working on the Sabbath, and so on. The researchers later decided that this high level of specificity was creating unnecessary confusion for respondents, leading the more detailed versions of these questions to be dropped.

For some innovations, ambiguity was created by differences between what might or might not have been voted on and decided by a formal body of the kibbutz, and what was actually happening on the kibbutz. One example was a question about whether kibbutz members were free to take jobs outside the kibbutz. Allowing members to work outside was originally treated as a decision that could only be made by the General Assembly of the kibbutz; the survey therefore at first asked respondents whether the kibbutz encouraged its members to work outside. Respondents later began to report that members were working outside, without being formally encouraged to do so; this led the researchers to drop the original question, after 1998, from the survey.

A question that asked about increases in the use of hired labor had similar problems. Some kibbutzim formally voted to increase their use of hired labor. Other kibbutzim hired more nonmembers without voting to do so. When a question about hired labor was added to the survey in 1993, it asked whether the kibbutz had voted to increase the use of hired labor. By the time this question was asked for the last time, in 1998, respondents were explaining negative answers by adding that hired labor was increasing, but no one had voted on the matter, or that hired labor could not increase further, because it was already very high.

Questions about compensation for work also had validity problems, but were too important to drop. From the beginning, the survey asked whether the kibbutz had "compensation for work," which meant payment on the basis of work, as opposed to the traditional kibbutz practice of payment on the basis of need. In 1995, a so-called mixed model began to be promoted, leading the Institute to split the question about compensation in two, with a new question explicitly aimed at mixed systems of compensation. In the years 1996–1998, many kibbutz secretaries who responded to the survey misunderstood the distinction between these two questions. They would answer yes, we have a mixed system of compensation, and yes, we pay differential salaries. The Institute later added an explanation of the difference between the mixed model and differential salaries to instructions accompanying the questions. As the terms *safety-net budget* and *mixed model* came into wide use, these errors became less frequent, but, in the years from 1996 to 1998, many errors were made in responding to these questions.

By the year 2001, the survey began to encounter more severe problems. Questions and answers began to take on different meanings, depending on whether they were asked in a collective or in a renewed kibbutz. For example, the question about whether members paid for meals in the dining hall had different meanings on the two types of kibbutzim. On a collective kibbutz, the answer that members did not pay for meals signified that all members continued to eat in the kibbutz dining hall without being charged; on a renewed kibbutz, that members did not pay for meals probably meant the kibbutz had closed its dining hall.

Many other questions began to take on differing meanings in the two types of kibbutzim. These included questions about arrangements for paying for education, and questions about pensions. This problem led the Institute to begin conducting separate surveys of collective and renewed kibbutzim, beginning in 2002. These separate surveys of the two populations did not produce as high a response rate as had the surveys of all kibbutzim, and they were soon terminated.

All this left 1990 through 2001 as the years in which a common series of questions about innovations was asked of all kibbutzim.

In motivating kibbutzim to respond to its survey, the Institute for Research of the Kibbutz at the University of Haifa had the benefit of being able to say that the survey was cosponsored by the kibbutz federations. In the first year, a second copy of the survey was sent out a month after the first. In later years, the questionnaire was sent out three times. In most years, as shown in table 2.1, nearly two hundred or more kibbutzim responded to the survey every year, producing response rates of nearly 80 percent or better.

Questionnaires were addressed to the general secretary of each kibbutz. Respondents filling out the questionnaire were asked to report their job title, and in most cases it was, as requested, the general secretary who completed the questionnaire.

The Process of Innovation

Because some reforms had already begun to spread in the late 1980s, researchers at the Institute knew that the introduction of change on the kibbutzim was a long and slow process. First, an administrator, such as the secretary or some other person in a decision-making position would propose a change to a colleague. Then they would decide whether or not to propose it to the members. Before a change could be presented to the members, it needed to be turned into a specific proposal, with details about how much it would cost and how it woul be paid for. The process would remain informal until someone started writing these matters down. Then the committee responsible would prepare the proposal to present to the members for a vote. At this point it was an official proposal.

Because many of the proposed changes included in the survey were highly significant and controversial, researchers wanted not only to know how many kibbutzim had already introduced a given innovation, but also to know how many kibbutzim were in the process of introducing that innovation, or were even talking about it. So, in addition to offering a kibbutz secretary the opportunity to indicate that their kibbutz was "not considering" or was "already using" an innovation, the survey offered "we are discussing it," "we have decided to do it," and "we are implementing it" as alternative responses, along with "we have rejected it."

Instructions that accompanied the questionnaire included explanations of what was intended by the words "discussing," "rejected," "decided," "implementing," and "using." In the early years of the survey, secretaries occasionally volunteered remarks that made possible improvements to these explanations in subsequent years. For example, to say that a kibbutz was in the process of "implementing" a change, it was clarified, the kibbutz needed to be within two years of actually using the change.

In the first year of the survey, some secretaries reported that their kibbutzim were "discussing" an innovation, but would add that kibbutz members were speaking about it only informally: "in the street," at the worksite, and so on. In the second year, the questionnaire specified that to be considered under "discussion," a proposal had to have been discussed by some formal body of the kibbutz, such as a committee or the General Assembly. The questionnaire did not ask respondents to specify which body was "discussing" a change, or had "rejected" it; so, in the case of these responses, it is possible that only a committee was involved. When respondents reported that a kibbutz had "decided" to introduce an innovation, acceptance could only have come from a body that had authority to accept, which normally meant the General Assembly.

In some years, the researchers added a seventh response category: that the kibbutz had abandoned the innovation after previously using it. It was later decided that this category was unnecessary, because abandonment could be inferred whenever a kibbutz reported that it was "not considering" an innovation, after previously having reported that it was "using" it.

Reports that a kibbutz had "decided" to use an innovation, was "implementing" the innovation, or was already "using" it, had similar, overlapping meanings. In some years, two or three questionnaires would be received from the same kibbutz, and they would give two or three different answers about which stage the kibbutz was at in the process, even when the same individual filled out the questionnaire each time.

In chapters 2, 3, and 4, three different strategies were used for minimizing the effects of respondents' potential confusion about differences among these response categories. Chapter 2 reports only the proportion of kibbutzim responding that they are currently "using" each innovation, and ignores all intermediate responses. Chapter 4 focuses on kibbutzim whose members have voted to transform the kibbutz into a kibbutz of a new type. For these analyses, differences between "decided," "implementing," and "using" are of no importance, because we combine these responses together to identify "renewed" kibbutzim.

Of the three chapters that make use of these data, only chapter 3 looks closely at the ordinality among the responses, because it seeks to identify factors that make a kibbutz more or less likely to move toward or away from adoption on this six-part scale of responses. Before initiating these analyses, we deleted from the data set nine questions that produced unusually high numbers of inconsistent responses from year to year. After these nine problematic questions had been eliminated, the forty-two questions that remained showed a reasonably high consistency of responses from year to year, as shown in table A.1.

As discussed above, the nine questions that evoked inconsistent responses were generally questions that asked about the policy of the kibbutz toward a matter such as increasing the use of hired labor or allowing members to work outside rather than asking about the actual behavior of the kibbutz. One kibbutz secretary would respond by describing the policy of the kibbutz, but another would answer on the basis of what the kibbutz was actually doing. The nine innovations deleted from analyses of year-to-year changes in responses because of such problems were: replacing committees with officeholders; abolishing rotation of managers; using economic branches as profit centers; separating the economy from the community; allowing members to work outside the kibbutz; making finding their own work be the responsibility of members; replacing members with hired labor; increasing the use of hired labor; and closing services.

Although table A.1 confirms the ordinality among the responses "discussing," "decided," "implementing," and "using," this table reveals the response that a kibbutz has "rejected" an innovation to be problematic. Fewer than half of all reports that a kibbutz has rejected an innovation are repeated in the following year. The more frequent response in the year following reports of rejection is that the kibbutz is "not considering" the innovation. This suggests that the rejection of innovations is quickly forgotten, and that year-to-year transitions in responses from "rejected" to "not considering" are not likely to be meaningful. Fortunately, the response that a kibbutz has "rejected" an innovation is given infrequently, so this problem is not likely to have had an important effect on our statistical results.

Year-to-Year Changes in Responses

The analysis thus far has made inferences about the meaning of responses, based solely on a consideration of which innovations most frequently evoke each response. Another perspective on the meaning of each response can be obtained by comparing each first-year response to the response given by the same kibbutz to the same question in the following year.

Table A.1 matches responses given by each kibbutz to each question in each year, to the responses given by the same kibbutz to the same question in the following year. In each year, the table orders responses from "we have rejected it," the response most unfavorable to adoption, to "we are using it," the response most favorable to adoption. With six response categories in each year, there are thirty-six possible combinations of responses from year to year.

The highest probabilities reported in table A.1 appear on the diagonal line from the upper left to the lower right. These cells represent instances in which organizations gave the same response in two consecutive years. If the response in the previous year was "not considering," 77.3 percent of responding kibbutzim give that same response in the following year. If the response in the previous year was (currently) "using," 81.4 percent give that same response in the following year.

For the other four responses, probabilities appearing on the diagonal are substantially lower. For innovations "under discussion" in the first

TABLE A.1.

Probabilities of Transitions from Responses in

	Response in Later Year		
Response in earlier year	*Rejected*	*Not considering*	*Discussing*
Rejected	0.175	0.661	0.164
Not considering	0.012	0.773	0.134
Discussing	0.014	0.341	0.352
Decided to adopt	0.008	0.173	0.127
Implementing	0.007	0.148	0.127
Currently using	0.004	0.098	0.037

year, 35.2 percent give this same response in the second. For innovations reported as "rejected," "decided," or in the process of implementation, about one kibbutz in six give this same response in the following year. The low probabilities with which these responses are repeated from year to year indicate that these are clearly transitional responses, not stable states.

If these latter responses represent organizations in transition, what is the direction that the transitions take? The numbers shown in the upper right portion of table A.1 are estimates of probabilities of movements toward use of innovations. The numbers shown in the lower left are estimates of probabilities of movements away from use. If every innovation considered does sooner or later get adopted, then the probabilities in the upper right portion of table A.1 will be close to one, and those in the lower left will be near zero.

In table A.1, probabilities in the upper right are generally higher than those in the lower left. This was to be expected, given that the average prevalence of these innovations was rising during this period. But the risks of failure, estimated by the figures shown in the lower left portion of table A.1, are substantial at every stage.

For each of the six possible responses in year one, the last column of table A.1 reports probabilities that a kibbutz will be "using" the innovation in question in year two. Of kibbutzim reporting that they had "rejected" an innovation in the previous year, none reported in the next year that

Earlier Year to Responses in Later Year

	Response in Later Year		
Decided to adopt	*Implementing*	*Currently using*	*Number of cases*
0.000	0.000	0.000	372
0.011	0.014	0.055	20,964
0.053	0.073	0.167	4907
0.157	0.109	0.426	928
0.047	0.153	0.518	1,061
0.021	0.025	0.814	8,732

they were "using" this innovation. Columns four and five of table A.1 also indicate that no kibbutzim reporting that they had "rejected" an innovation report in the following year that they had "decided" on that innovation or were in the process of "implementing" it. Among kibbutzim reporting that they were "not considering" an innovation in the first year, on the other hand, the probabilities of all three of these transitions toward use of innovations are substantial. It is for this reason that table A.1 places "rejected" as the response most distant from current use of an innovation.

While "rejected" is clearly the most negative response, it is also among the least stable. Only 17.5 percent of kibbutzim reporting in the earlier year that they have "rejected" an innovation give this same response in the later year. A much greater proportion, 66.1 percent, report in the later year that they are "not considering" the innovation. In light of the rarity of transitions from rejection to use of innovations, it would be unwise to infer that the transition from "rejected" to "not considering" reflects a reduction in opposition to the given innovation on the given kibbutz. It seems instead that the term "rejected" is reserved for innovations about which votes or discussions have recently been held. When proposals to introduce innovations have been off the organization's agenda for more than a year, it becomes more common to report that the kibbutz is "not considering" it. This tendency for reports that an innovation has been rejected to transform themselves into reports that the innovation is not being considered may help to explain why reports that innovations have been rejected are relatively rare.

"Not considering" is the most common initial response, and it is a status from which transitions to all other states are possible. Although much research on diffusion of innovations treats the transition from "not considering" to currently "using" as occurring instantaneously, organizations whose initial response was "not considering" are much more likely to report in the second year that they are "discussing" the innovation (13.4 percent) than that they are currently "using" it (5.5 percent).

The response that an innovation is under discussion is shown by its consequences to be the most equivocal response. Organizations reporting that they are "discussing" an innovation in the first year are equally likely to report in the next year that they are no longer considering the innovation, or have accepted it, or are still discussing it.

Of the remaining transitional responses, reports that innovations have been decided or are in the process of implementation are the two most likely to be followed by reports of current use. But even at these late stages, success is by no means assured. In only about half of all cases do organizations reporting in the prior year that innovations have been "decided" or are in process of implementation report in the next year that the innovation is currently in use.

Thus when a kibbutz reports that a given innovation is under discussion, has been decided, or in the process of implementation, this does not mean that the kibbutz has embarked on a path that will make it a user of that innovation within one or two years. Rather, these responses are signs that the innovation has encountered some kind of trouble. They represent ways in which efforts to introduce innovations can become bogged down or derailed, not orderly steps in a process whose outcome is predetermined.

If discussion, decision, and implementation are hazards to be avoided rather than steps that all decisions must go through, it becomes interesting to ask about the circumstances under which they can be avoided. The probabilities reported in table A.1 suggest that few efforts to introduce innovations go through all of these stages, but most go through at least one of them. Among kibbutzim reporting in the earlier year that they were not considering an innovation, only 5.5 percent report in the next year that they are currently using the innovation, versus 13.4 percent who say that the innovation is now under discussion, and smaller proportions reporting that the innovation has been decided (1.1 percent) or is in the process of implementation (1.4 percent). Added together, the frequencies of these three indirect paths from not considered toward adoption outnumber the probability of the direct path by 15.9 percent to 5.5 percent, or about three to one.

The innovations that most frequently take the less typical direct path from "not considered" to "current use" are all innovations that tables 2.2–2.6 identify as being among the most widely adopted innovations. The literature on the diffusion of innovations in organizations suggests that, as more organizations adopt an innovation, the example they set facilitates the introduction of the same innovation in the remaining organizations by offering models to imitate (AhmadJian and Robinson 2001; DiMaggio and Powell 1983). The availability of such models could shorten the amount of time required both to identify alternatives and to implement chosen courses of action. It is also possible that the ability to introduce these changes quickly without going through long and hazardous periods of discussion and implementation contributes to their widespread acceptance.

The bottom line of table A.1 indicates that innovations continue to be exposed to the risk of failure, even after they have been adopted. Only 81.4 percent of kibbutzim reporting that they are using an innovation in any given year give this same response in the next year. Of the 18.6 percent that give other responses in the second year, 2.1 percent report that the innovation has been decided upon but not yet implemented, and 2.5 percent report that the change is in the process of implementation. Since these three responses all imply approval of an innovation, and differ only in what they imply about the extent of progress in implementation, we cannot treat transitions among these categories as evidence of failure of innovations. That leaves 14 percent of kibbutzim previously reporting use of an innovation giving responses that indicate that they have later abandoned the innovation: 9.8 percent reporting that they are not considering the innovation, 3.7 percent reporting that they are discussing it, and 0.4 percent reporting that they have rejected it.

The literature on the diffusion of innovations in organizations focuses on the adoption of changes by organizations, and rarely considers the possibility that innovations once adopted will later be abandoned. Against the backdrop of the general silence of the literature on the subject, the rate of abandonment of innovations observed here seems surprisingly high. That makes it necessary to try to identify factors that cause the rate of abandonment among these innovations to be so high.

It is possible that an unknown portion of the instances of abandonment observed here may be attributable to errors made by informants. If the rate of errors by respondents in individual years were as high as 10 percent, the frequency of errors in two-year pairs of observations would be sufficient to produce the rate of abandonment reported. A more thorough discussion of the validity of responses appeared above, but here we summarize the most important considerations leading us to believe that this high apparent rate of abandonment of innovations is not primarily attributable to errors by respondents.

Before initiating these analyses, we compared all questions on the frequency with which a question produced consistent or inconsistent responses from year to year. This analysis identified nine questions that produced unusually high frequencies of changes in responses from year to year. We concluded that the inconsistencies in responses to these items were due to ambiguities in the items themselves, and excluded them from the analyses reported here. These ambiguous questions often asked about the policies of a kibbutz, rather than about its actual practices, allowing one respondent to report what the kibbutz intended, while another reported what it actually did. After these ambiguous items had been eliminated, most remaining questions dealt with explicit practices about which kibbutz members could be expected to be well informed.

Our second reason for placing confidence in the estimates of the probability of year-to-year transitions reported in table A.1 is that they are very different from the random pattern that a set of erroneous responses would produce. For example, although 23.9 percent of responses indicated that a kibbutz was currently using an innovation, in none of the 372 instances in which a kibbutz reported in the first year that it had rejected an innovation did it report in the next year that it was currently using it. Similarly, although "not considering" and "currently using" were the two most numerous categories, direct transitions from "not considering" to "currently using" were much less common than indirect transitions.

Finally, we are inclined to accept reports of the abandonment of innovations as valid, because of the way they are distributed among innovations. Of the ten most frequently retained innovations, two increased the income of the kibbutz by opening kibbutz housing and educational services to outsiders. Most of the rest reduced kibbutz costs by privatizing expenditures. Innovations like pension plans and metering members' use of electricity involved long-term commitments and sunk costs that would make them hard to undo.

In identifying instances of apparent abandonment of innovations, we include all instances in which an innovation was reported in the initial year of a pair as being in use but was reported in the following year as not in use. The two most frequently abandoned innovations are two changes whose legitimacy was vigorously contested throughout the period under review: payment of differential salaries to members, and selling houses to nonmembers. Only in 2005 did the kibbutz movements and the Israeli government formally grant to the kibbutzim the right to make such substantial departures from their traditionally collective structures and practices. Until such authorization was granted, there was a great deal of uncertainty about whether kibbutzim had the right to introduce such radical changes and continue to call themselves kibbutzim. Transfers of ownership of land from the kibbutzim to nonmembers required the approval of the Israeli government, and such approval was not given before 2005. The uncertainty surrounding these innovations is reflected in the fact that in 100 percent of the instances in which a kibbutz reported that it was already engaging in either of these practices, in the following year it reported that it had merely decided to introduce the change, or was in the process of implementing it, or was discussing taking this action.

In the case of other innovations, the considerations leading to abandonment may be more practical than institutional. Partnerships with private investors depend upon the ability of the kibbutz to find suitable investors to partner with. Establishing connections between days worked and members' budgets, and including expenses for higher education and other enrichments for children in parents' budgets, both assume that members continue to receive need-based budgets from the kibbutz. As kibbutzim began to abandon need-based budgets for systems of differential salaries, these innovations in the traditional budgetary system of the kibbutzim quickly became obsolete.

Insofar as reports of the abandonment of innovations can be taken as valid, they further demonstrate the uncertainty that was present at every stage of the consideration and implementation of the innovations by the kibbutzim during these years. Proposals for reform were at risk of failure at every stage, even after innovations were put into use.

Measures in the Statistical Analyses

The statistical models in tables A.3, A.4, and A.7 use a number of variables to test hypotheses about the causes of adoption of innovations and of transitions to the renewed form.

Movement toward or from Adopting Innovations

In the 1990–2001 surveys of innovations, respondents were asked to report, for each innovation, whether their kibbutz were not considering the innovation, had considered and rejected it, were discussing it, had decided to adopt it, were in the process of implementing it, or were currently using it. Table A.1 compares the response of a kibbutz to any given question in one year to the response of the same kibbutz to the same question in the following year. As table A.1 demonstrates, these two-year pairs of responses can be ordered from movement away from using the innovation (i.e., toward rejection of it) to movement toward using it. Any movement from "using" was coded as movement "away." If an innovation was in the process of implementation at the beginning of a period, movement to using the innovation was coded as movement "toward" and any other change as movement "away." For cases that had "decided" at the beginning of the spell of observation, movement to "implementing" or "using" was coded as "toward" and any other change was coded as "away." For those who had "rejected" at the beginning of the spell, any movement was regarded as "toward" with the exception of "not considered" (this was treated as no change in status). For cases discussing an innovation at the origin time, "rejection" or "not considering" subsequently was regarded as movement "away" from using the innovation, with all other changes coded as movements "toward" using it. For cases that were "not considering" an innovation at the beginning of the period, any movement except "rejection" was treated as a movement "toward" use. Each observation was coded simply according to whether the subsequent survey reported no change in status (N = 25,666 or 69.4 percent), a movement away from use (N = 4,248 or 11.5 percent), or a movement toward use (N = 7,050 or 19.1 percent).

Type of Budget

In table A.7, we examine the effects of a number of variables on the log-odds that the compensation system of a kibbutz is of the "mixed" or "safety-net" form, relative to the traditional "need-based" system. Because both the kibbutz federations and the Institute for Research of the Kibbutz have recognized from the very beginning the potential for these innovations to change the identity of a kibbutz, they have closely watched such innovations.

For the Institute, the surveys of kibbutzim that it conducted annually from 1990 through 2001 have served as its primary source of information about compensation systems in use on individual kibbutzim in those years. Insofar as information provided by a kibbutz about compensation was missing or inconsistent, the Institute contacted the kibbutz to complete or correct the data. Since 2002, data on kibbutz types have been provided by the kibbutz movement, supplemented by fax surveys sent annually by the Institute to all need-based and mixed kibbutzim asking them if they have changed to another type. Because the Institute has complete information about kibbutz type for all kibbutzim for all years since 1989, analyses of transitions among types of kibbutzim are conducted using a data set that begins with observations of all kibbutzim in all years, and is constrained only by the availability of data on covariates.

In the analysis of the likelihood that a kibbutz would be "safety-net" or "mixed" relative to "need-based," the proportion of all kibbutzim that had already made a transition of form was included as an independent variable. The percentage of kibbutzim that were "mixed" or "safety-net" in the pooled sample ranged from 0.0 percent to 69.4 percent, with a mean of 21.7 percent and a standard deviation of 24.8 percent.

Economic Crisis

In the analyses shown in tables A.3, A.4, and A.7, the economic performance of a kibbutz is used as a predictor of the likelihood that it will move toward or away from implementing innovations, and of the likelihood that it will adopt the "mixed" and "safety net" forms. As part of the restructuring of kibbutz finances that occurred in the late 1980s, an evaluation of the economic condition of all kibbutzim was conducted in 1988. A subsequent evaluation was performed in 1994, and since 1997 annual evaluations have been conducted and reported. The methodology for evaluating the economic condition of the kibbutz is somewhat complex. It includes consideration of debt loads, cash flow, and assets, following generally accepted accounting approaches for financial audits of businesses. Details of the methodology are reported in Yoffe (2005).

We faced a number of significant challenges in assembling useable data on the economic condition of the kibbutzim. For the period before 1997, we had only two reports (1988 and 1994), and these rated the kibbutzim on a scale of economic crisis from 1 for kibbutzim "in very good economic condition" to 5 for kibbutzim "in very bad economic condition." For the period from 1997 onward, reports were not complete, and some missing observations needed to be imputed.

In the period before 1995, the economic-condition score from the 1988 survey was used; in the period for 1995 and 1996, the 1994 report was used. These ratings were rescaled from their original 1–5 scores to a new scale ranging from 0–100, corresponding to the data from 1997 onward. The economic condition (EC) data for 1994 showed: 1 (excellent condition) = 11 percent, 2 = 22 percent, 3 = 9 percent, 4 = 24 percent, 5 = 17 percent (worst condition). Using the 1997 new data, a percentile distribution roughly matching this 1–5 scale was obtained by using the cutoffs: 1 = (20 to 40) (there are few, if any, cases rated better than 20 in any year), 2 = (40 to 60), 3 = (60 to 70), 4 = (70 to 80), 5 = 80 and above (the maximum is 95 to 98, in most years). The midpoints of these intervals were used to recode the EC scores prior to the new 1997 data: 1 = 30, 2 = 50, 3 = 65, 4 = 75, 5 = 90.

This method of rescoring the limited reports on economic condition prior to 1997 results in restricted variation in this variable, for the earlier period of time. From the existing data, it does appear that economic condition changes rather slowly and monotonically for most kibbutzim. The crude estimates before 1997 are likely to result in attenuated estimates of the effects of economic condition on outcomes, but are probably broadly valid assessments of the differences among the kibbutzim.

In the period from 1997 onward, annual reports were available, and were scored on a 0 to 100 scale. Unfortunately, 5 percent of the observations were missing, and imputations were made to produce a complete panel. The following rules were used to impute missing economic condition scores. Rule 1: If 2005 is missing, but 2004 is present, impute the 2005 value by using the 2004 value (30 imputations). Rule 2: If 1997 is missing but 1998 is present, impute 1998 value to 1997 (2 imputations). Rule 3: If any single observation is missing, but the two adjacent observations are present, impute the missing value as the arithmetic average of adjacent values (18 imputations). Rule 4: If missing more than one value at the beginning of the series, but later data are present, impute by a constant equal to the first available value (4 imputations). Rule 5: If missing more than one value in the middle of the period, impute the missing values as the arithmetic average of the values before and after the missing values (29 imputations). Rule 6: If missing two or more observations at the end of the series, but earlier data are present, impute as a constant at the last observed value (2 imputations). Rule 7: If missing all observations, impute with the mean value for each year (27 imputations). In general, these rules have the consequence of reducing variation, and hence probably attenuating relationships with this variable.

Size and Change in Size

The size of a kibbutz at the time of an observation is defined as the count of its members. Annual data on membership was obtained from the kibbutz federations.

It should be noted that the membership of the kibbutz and the number of persons resident at the kibbutz are not necessarily the same; this is increasingly true toward the present time. Early in the period, virtually all kibbutz members were resident full-time at the settlements; later in the time period, some members (primarily those holding employment away from the kibbutz) might not be regularly in residence. Early in the period, there were few nonmembers present at the kibbutzim (though there were often visitors at some kibbutzim); in recent years, a number of kibbutzim provide facilities for short or extended residence by nonmembers.

When size is used as a predictor variable in our analyses, it is number of members, rather than number of residents, that is considered. Only members participate in the processes determining organizational change, and theories of the effects of size refer primarily to the size of the community's membership. In the samples used in our analyses, the mean number of members ranges between 210 and 235, with standard deviations of about 130.

In the analyses of causes of the adoption of innovations, as well as of the "safety-net" budget, change in membership size from year to year is used as a predictor variable. For these analyses, change in size is the difference between the number of members at the year of observation of the dependent variable, and at the previous year. In all analyses of change in size, the raw number of the difference in membership is used (rather than the percentage change in size). Since the absolute size measure is also included in all of these analyses, the coefficient of change in size (or the effects of other variables on change in size) needs to be interpreted as relative to the absolute size of the membership. In the sample used to analyze movement toward or away from the adoption of individual innovations, and in the sample used to predict the adoption of the mixed or safety-net budgets, the mean change in size from year to year was -1.6 members, with a standard deviation of 8.7 members. The overall distribution of the variable is approximately normal, with considerable kurtosis.

Age and Age-Squared

Age is the number of years that have passed (at the time of observation of a dependent variable) since the kibbutz was founded. For the kibbutzim that were formed early, there may be some ambiguity about the time at which these communities became kibbutzim in a formal sense; the nature and definition of the kibbutz was in considerable flux in the early years (see discussion in chapter 1). We have used the date at which a community was formed, which is the date that the kibbutz movement generally recognizes as the founding date. Data on these dates of formation were provided by the Institute for Research of the Kibbutz, which took them from its records. In the samples used in our analyses, the mean age observed is slightly over 50 years, with a standard deviation of approximately 15 years.

Some hypotheses suggest that the effect of age on outcomes may be nonlinear, composed of both a linear and a parabolic (threshold) component. To test these hypotheses, the age variable is squared and divided by 100 (to make the regression coefficients of this term more interpretable).

Federation

Until their recent merger, the kibbutzim studied here were affiliated with either Takam or the Artzi Federation. We have consistently excluded from our analyses a small number (16) of kibbutzim that are affiliated with a conservative religious federation. The choice of affiliation, we believe, indicates a more (Artzi) or less (Takam) traditional ideology toward the kibbutz as an institution. The federations (particularly Artzi) may also make suggestions regarding, and have influence over, the pace and form of innovation of their members. Kibbutzim affiliated with the more ideologically coherent Artzi Federation are coded 1 in our statistical models and constitute one-third of the observations, and those affiliated with the larger and more permissive Takam Federation (constituting about two-thirds of our observations) are coded 0 (and, consequently, are treated as the reference group). The regression coefficients for federation, then, should be interpreted as differences of Artzi-affiliated kibbutzim from Takam-affiliated kibbutzim, controlling for other factors in the model.

Percentage Adopting Each Innovation

In our analyses of movement toward or away from the adoption of innovations, the proportion of other kibbutzim that have already adopted the
innovation plays a key role. To determine the percentage of kibbutzim that
have adopted an innovation, we count only the kibbutzim reporting that
they are currently using the innovation, and divide this number by the total
of all kibbutzim responding regarding that innovation in the given year.
This rate is then used to predict rates of transition from the current year
of observation to the next. The percent adopting has a mean value of 23.6
percent, with relatively high variability (standard deviation = 22.4 percent).

Geographic Isolation

To test Kanter's (1972) prediction that geographic isolation makes communes less likely to change, we measure the distance of each kibbutz (in
kilometers) from Tel Aviv or Haifa, whichever is nearer, following the standard practice of Israel's Central Bureau of Statistics. It should be noted that
a small number of kibbutzim (no more than a dozen) are closer to Jerusalem than to either of the two larger cities. The special character of Jerusalem, however, may make it less significant as a source of "modernism"
than are the other cities. The mean distance from cities in our samples is
approximately 75 km, with a standard deviation of 55–60 km.

Prior Experience with Innovations

In the analysis of movements toward the adoption of innovations, and in
the analysis of the adoption of the "renewed" form, prior experience with
other innovations is hypothesized to increase the likelihood of further
change. The prior experience index is an effort to indicate the cumulative experience of each kibbutz with the adoption of innovations at the
beginning of each period of observation. Two problems arose in measuring prior experience. First, not all innovations were assessed in each of the
annual surveys. Second, in some areas (e.g., collective or individualized
consumption) more innovations were assessed than in other areas (e.g.,
changes in compensation).

The index was constructed by first dividing all of the innovations that
appeared on the survey at any point into one of four categories: a) material

incentives (includes: connecting days worked and budget, additional budget due to seniority, payment for work on the Sabbath, payment for additional work in services, payment for seasonal work in guis, reduced pay for reduced days worked, and additional pay for additional days worked); b) privatization of consumption (includes: pay for meals, pay for electricity, pay for recreation, pay for overseas travel, right to own or use a private car, increase size of house at own expense, comprehensive budget, higher education in the member's budget, privatization of education, parents' budget that includes enrichment, special expenses for children in parents' budget, privatization of health services, privatizing of the laundry); c) closing or cutting back services (includes: canceling breakfast in dining hall, canceling evening meal in dining hall, closing of services, closing the dining hall); and d) all other innovations.

For each year, for each of the four broad categories of innovations, for each kibbutz, the percentage of the possible innovations that were reported "in use" was tallied. These percentages were then summed across the categories of innovation types. The cumulative index of prior experience with innovations was then created by summing the scores for all years prior to the year of a given observation, for each kibbutz. The resulting index values range from zero (prior to any adoptions) to 266.6.

In the construction of the annual surveys, some innovations that had already been very widely adopted were dropped. Over the period of study, a substantial number of new innovations arose, and were added to the survey only for the later years. Dropping already widely adopted innovations had the effect of reducing the cumulative prior experience index; adding new and not widely adopted innovations may also have had this effect. The index, then, probably understates the extent of prior experience with innovations. Since all kibbutzim are affected equally, however, no bias is introduced. Since the index is cumulative, total prior experience must remain constant or increase over time for any kibbutz.

Statistical Analyses

In chapter 3, we focused on the process of adoption of individual innovations. For these analyses, the unit of observation was the status of an innovation in a pair of adjacent years, nested within kibbutz, innovation, and time. In chapter 4, we focused on the transition of the kibbutz from "need-based" budgets to "mixed" or "safety-net" budgetary forms. For these analyses, the data consist of a panel of kibbutzim by year. These models are discussed in some detail below.

The pooling of observations over years, kibbutzim, and innovations raises some statistical issues. The estimates of standard errors of effects (and, hence, tests of significance) in the software used assume independent random sampling. Two observations from the same kibbutz are likely to be more similar than two observations from kibbutzim drawn at random; two observations from the same year are likely to be more similar than observations from two years drawn at random. Failure to account for all these forms of nonindependence of observations may result in estimates of standard errors that are too small. Incorrectly small estimates of standard errors can lead to "false positive" results for testing hypotheses that independent variables have impacts on dependent variables. That is, we may conclude that x affects y, when in fact it does not.

There are a variety of commonly used approaches for dealing with nonindependence in pooled data (Rabe-Hesketh and Skrondal 2008). The most straightforward (and the approach adopted here) are "fixed effects" models in which the analyst supposes that there may be systematic differences in outcomes for each case (i.e., kibbutz) and each time point (i.e., year of observation). Vectors of binary variables representing each kibbutz and each year are entered into the prediction equations along with the other independent variables. This adjusts for differences in the average outcome that are unique to a particular kibbutz (but common across time), or to a particular time point (but common across kibbutzim). A more elaborate, but fairly similar approach is called GEE (generalized estimating equations). In GEE analysis, the nonindependence of observations is treated as patterns of residual variance and covariance. The residuals (that is, variance due to sources other than the observed independent variables) are decomposed into random error and systematic error due to kibbutz and time. This approach allows that the effects of nonindependence in time may be random, or (commonly) serially correlated; it also allows that the error variance of each case (kibbutz) may differ. Experiments with our data suggested that there were few meaningful differences between fixed-effects and GEE models under most reasonable assumptions about error structures. Consequently, the more straightforward fixed-effects results are reported in this text.

A third approach to panel data is also possible. One can conceive of the data as observations of outcomes that constitute growth curves (multiple observations of outcomes over time) that occur within each of a large number of "populations" of cases defined by kibbutzim (Littell et al. 1996; Twisk 2003). The "mixed model" or "hierarchical model" approach essentially estimates models as time series within each kibbutz and then averages the results. This type of hierarchical approach makes logical sense, but is very demanding in terms of replications and distributional assumptions. Since our analysis does not emphasize the importance of cross-level interactions, we preferred more robust fixed-effects analysis.

Modeling the Adoption of Innovations

Chapter 3 focused on processes that led kibbutzim to move toward or away from the use of a number of specific innovations from one year to the next. Using data from the annual surveys of the kibbutzim, the analysis excluded nine innovations whose measurement was determined to be problematic as discussed above, and omitted all other innovations that were observed only for a single year between 1991 and 2001, leaving 42 innovations with valid year-to-year pairs of observations. Some of these innovations were not included in the survey each year; those that had been widely adopted were dropped from the survey; and a number of new innovations were added in later years, leading to an incomplete panel design. In addition, not all kibbutzim responded to the survey in all years, resulting in a further loss of observations. Since our analysis was based on observation of movement toward or away from use of innovations, cases were lost to analysis if they were not observed in both of each pair of adjacent years. The final sample size for the analysis of movements toward or away from use of innovations was 36,964.

Tables A.3 and A.4 present models that analyze the effects of independent variables on the probability that a kibbutz at a particular stage in the adoption process in a given year moves toward or away from implementing each of a number of innovations in the subsequent year. Models are estimated separately for each initial status (i.e., "rejected," "not considering," "discussing," "decided," "implementing," or "using" at the beginning of the period). The models presented are multinomial logistic regressions, in which the generalized log odds of movement toward or away from implementation are expressed relative to the outcome of no change. This approach enables examination of the effects of independent variables on the probability of movement toward or away from adoption, given the status of implementation at time of examination. Estimates by maximum likelihood are obtained from the nominal regression routines of Statistical Package for the Social Sciences (SPSS) for Windows.

For our analyses, data are formed as a pool of observations across years, innovations, and kibbutzim. Not all innovations were observed in all years for all kibbutzim. Some innovations were dropped in later years, after they were widely diffused, while other innovations were added in later years. In addition, not all kibbutzim responded each year. To be included in the analysis, valid responses about the state of adoption of a particular innovation in adjacent years were needed. If all 250 nonreligious kibbutzim had responded to every question in every year in which it was asked, the cumulative total of observations would have reached 64,320. The actual total of observations available for these analyses is 33,983, a response rate of 52.8 percent. The loss of data due to each instance of nonresponse is high, because two observations are lost for each year that is missing, due to our need to organize observations into two-year pairs.

The large sample size (33,983) results from observations across multiple innovations in multiple years for each of the kibbutzim. Consequently, the observations are (potentially) nonindependent due to pooling time, pooling innovations, and pooling kibbutzim. We adopted a number of procedures intended to address these sources of nonindependence.

The effects of pooling across years are addressed in two ways. First, the models that we present include a vector of fixed intercepts for each year; this adjustment corrects for year-to-year changes in the innovations included in the survey, differences in respondents in a given year, and any random time-specific shocks. Second, we include the proportion of observations that have already adopted each innovation in the year prior as a predictor of current transition probabilities. Third, the observations that are at each stage of adoption at the beginning of a period are analyzed as separate populations. The inclusion of this prior adoption rate and of stratified analysis of populations defined by origin status should remove autoregression in the error term.

The effects of pooling across innovations and across kibbutzim are addressed through the inclusion of predictors that capture the main sources of commonality across them. It was not feasible to include fixed effects for kibbutz and for innovation due to sparseness of the data in many parts of the design. Instead, we sought to explicitly model the main sources of common variance in innovations, and in kibbutzim directly. In the case of innovations, models include whether an innovation is of one of five major types (represented with dummy variables). It is reasonable to assume that the same unmeasured factors are more likely to affect the adoption of innovations of the same general type in common ways than any two randomly chosen innovations. This approach, however, does not capture effects of unmeasured variables on the unique features of each particular innovation. In the case of kibbutzim, models include such attributes as size, age, economic condition, membership change, federation, and location. It is possible that features of an individual kibbutz (e.g., its specific history, economic activities, local culture) may introduce some uncontrolled nonindependence among the histories of adoption of the multiple innovations within that kibbutz. These approaches probably do not provide a complete solution to the pooling problem, and caution is needed in the interpretation of levels of statistical significance, which are probably somewhat overstated in the tables.

Also included in our models for predicting movement toward or away from adoption of individual innovations is a term measuring the cumulative prior experience of each kibbutz in adopting innovations (see the discussion of the development of this index, earlier in this appendix). We hypothesized that kibbutzim may differ, due to local history and culture, in their global propensity to innovate. To the extent that this is true, the cumulative experience index may capture unobserved, kibbutz-specific, heterogeneity. The cumulative experience index is also included, because we hypothesize the development of an institutionalization of change to varying degrees within each of the kibbutzim. Prior high rates of change, we hypothesize, are indicative of an institutionalization of change (i.e., acceptance of change as normal and as valuable in itself). Past change, by this logic, should predict higher probabilities of change in the present moment. Recent work by Beck,

Brüderl, and Woywode (2008) leads to caution in making this interpretation, however; in brief, these authors suggest that unobserved organization-
specific propensity to change, and the "momentum" effect of prior change,
are difficult to distinguish; they find that momentum effects are, in some
studies, really due to constant organization-specific unmeasured heterogeneity. Without the inclusion of a specific fixed effect for each kibbutz, the
two interpretations cannot be safely parsed.

Covariates of Innovations, 1990–2001

Correlations for all predictors included in the analyses of the adoption of
innovations are shown in table A.2. The average kibbutz during this period
had 234 members and had been in existence for about fifty years. Size
and age are highly correlated (.60). Kibbutzim belonging to the Artzi Federation constitute 34 percent of the total. The average kibbutz is located
seventy-five kilometers from the nearest large city (Tel Aviv or Haifa). Rural

TABLE A.2.

Descriptive Statistics for Covariates of Innovations, 1990–2001

	1	*2*	*3*
1. Size	1.00		
2. Age	.60	1.00	
3. Age squared (/1000)	.58	.97	1.00
4. Economic crisis	-.33	-.15	-.16
5. Change in membership	.07	.01	-.01
6. Artzi federation	.13	.05	.04
7. Geographic isolation	-.28	-.42	-.37
8. Prior innovations	-.13	.12	.12
9. Proportion using	-.01	.02	.02
10. New rights and entitlements	.00	-.00	-.00
11. Differentiation and rationalization	.00	-.01	-.06
12. Involvement of nonmembers	-.05	.01	.01
13. Privatization of services	.00	-.01	-.01
14. Material rewards and incentives	-.04	.01	.02

kibbutzim are on average younger (-.42) and smaller (-.28) than other kibbutzim. The incidence of economic crisis is negatively correlated with both size (-.33) and age (-.15), indicating that older and larger kibbutzim are on average in better economic condition than younger and smaller ones.

Transitions toward Innovations

Estimates of the effects of each potential influence on transitions toward use of innovations are shown in table A.3. From both theoretical and practical points of view, the two-year pairs of greatest interest are those that begin with the response that the kibbutz is "not considering" the innovation, and end with responses that the kibbutz is "discussing," "preparing," or "using" the innovation. Fortunately, observations that begin with the response that the kibbutz is "not considering" the innovation are also the most numerous response pairs. The large number of observations that begin with "not considering" makes this the best opportunity to estimate

4	5	6	7	8	9	Mean	S.D.
						234.21	128.53
						49.84	14.35
						2.69	1.38
1.00						61.87	18.97
-.02	1.00					-.01	.08
.00	.06	1.00				.34	
-.10	.03	-.16	1.00			75.06	54.24
.19	-.04	-.22	-.13	1.00		336.28	278.79
.01	.02	-.01	.00	.11	1.00	23.62	22.39
-.00	-.01	.00	.00	-.02	.23	.06	
-.00	-.00	-.00	-.00	-.02	-.06	.19	
.00	.01	.00	-.00	.03	.16	.22	
-.00	-.01	-.00	.00	-.04	.06	.38	
.01	.01	.00	.00	.06	-.35	.15	

TABLE A.3.

Effects on the Probability of Moving toward the Use of Innovations

	Rejected	Not considering	Discussing	Decided	In process	In use
			Status in earlier year			
Size	.272*	.016	.100*	-.161	-.004	——
Age	-.107	-.024*	-.040*	.045	-.071	——
Age squared	1.005	.164*	.279	-.272	.656	——
Economic crisis	.011	.006*	.003	-.006	-.003	——
Change in membership	-.069	-3.189*	-1.035	3.243*	.398	——
Artzi federation	.554	-.120*	-.245*	-.316	-.188	——
Distance from cities	-.007	-.002*	.000	-.003	.004	——
Prior innovations	.001	.001*	.000	.000	.000	——
Proportion using	.032*	.029*	.023*	.021*	.021*	——
Differentiation and rationalization	.166	-.180*	.238	-.194	.438	——
Involvement of nonmembers	-.692	-.620*	.201	-.049	-.071	——
Privatization of services	-1.089	-.908*	.538*	.542	-.168	——
Material rewards and incentives	-.322	-.488*	-.577*	2.315*	.278	——
N	372.000	17.915.000	4.907.000	928.000	939.000	7,806.000
Naglekerke R-squared	.163	.129	.126	.138	.119	.059

* $p < .05$ one-tailed. Size is measured in 100s of members. Age squared is measured in thousands. Age squared is measured in thousands.

Reference category for type of innovation is "New rights and entitlements."

the unique effects of each of the potential influences listed on the left side of table A.3.

The column labeled "not considering" in table A.3 indicates that most of the variables included have the effects expected for them, with the exception of size and age. Although size had appeared from the correlations to be negatively associated with the incidence of innovations, when all other influences had been taken into account, it had no net effect. The effects of age are curvilinear, as anticipated, but the curvilinearity observed is not what we anticipated. Instead of a positive effect of age on innovation signifying degeneration, and a negative effect for age-squared signifying regeneration, here the linear form of age has a negative effect on change, representing growing inertia over time, and age-squared, which represents the effects of higher values of age, has the positive effect on innovation predicted by theories of degeneration.

Economic crisis has a significantly positive effect on consideration of innovations (.006). This means that, as expected, kibbutzim that are in good economic condition are less likely to take steps toward adoption of innovations, and kibbutzim that are in economic difficulty are more likely to do so. Change in membership, as expected, has a negative effect on the probability that a kibbutz will start to consider an innovation (-3.189). Kibbutzim that are gaining members are less likely to consider innovations, and kibbutzim that are losing members are more likely to consider them. Both measures of resource scarcity thus behave as expected. These results are also consistent with the account of the origin of the reforms that was provided in chapter 2; if the current wave of reforms was instigated by a crisis that was both economic and demographic, we should not be surprised to find that the individual kibbutzim most likely to introduce these reforms are the ones that have been either losing money or losing members.

Federation and location also behave as expected. Artzi kibbutzim are less likely than Takam kibbutzim to consider innovations (-.120). Once innovations have been brought up for discussion, Artzi kibbutzim are significantly less likely that Takam kibbutzim to take further steps toward introducing the innovation (-.245). Remote locations make kibbutzim less likely to consider innovations (-.002). According to table A.4, kibbutzim that are far from cities are also more likely to abandon innovations once these are in the process of being implemented (.005).

Table A.3 provides evidence that the process of innovation feeds on itself in two distinct ways. Within individual kibbutzim, the more innovations a kibbutz has introduced in the past, the greater the likelihood that it will consider all remaining innovations (.001). Among the kibbutzim as a whole, the higher the proportion of kibbutzim that have already introduced an innovation, the greater the likelihood that the remaining kibbutzim will consider that innovation (.029).

Turning to the other columns of table A.3, the proportion of kibbutzim that are currently using the innovation is the only influence that consistently exerts significant effects at every stage. Of the remaining transitions modeled in table A.3, those that begin with "discussing" innovations are based on the largest number of observations (4,907). Yet even in the presence of this relatively high statistical power, most organizational characteristics lose significance at this stage. The exceptions are age of the kibbutz (-.040) and membership in the Artzi federation (-.245), which continue to have negative effects, and the size of the kibbutz, which at this stage acquires a positive effect (.100). In transitions that begin with reports that an innovation has been "decided," change in membership has an unanticipated positive effect on the probability of movement toward use (3.243). In modeling the probability of transitions from the process of implementation to actual use of innovations, the proportion of other kibbutzim currently using the innovation is the only predictor whose effect attains significance. Here, as at all other stages shown in table A.3, its effect is positive.

Transitions Away from Innovations

Models of transitions away from use of innovations are shown in table A.4. In these models, four predictors have significant and consistent effects at three or more stages. The proportion of other kibbutzim currently using an innovation has significantly negative effects on movements away from use of innovations at three of the five stages modeled: transitions beginning with reports that innovations were "not being considered" (-.013), were "under discussion" (-.010), or were "in use" (-.019). Successful introduction of prior innovations in the individual kibbutz also reduces the likelihood of movements away from use at three stages: among kibbutzim reporting that they were "discussing" the innovation (-.001), were in the process of "implementing" the innovation (-.001), or were "currently using"

TABLE A.4.

Effects on the Probability of Moving Away from the Use of Innovations

			Status in earlier year			
	Rejected	Not considering	Discussing	Decided	In process	In use
Size	—	-.144*	.025	.041	-.241*	-.085*
Age	—	.006	-.003	.062	-.049	-.009
Age squared	—	-.019	.028	-.397	.556	.128
Economic crisis	—	.007	-.004*	.004	-.004	.001
Change in membership	—	1.818	2.132*	3.538*	1.867	2.334*
Artzi federation	—	-.045	-.067	.081	-.191	.005
Distance from cities	—	-.001	-.001	.001	.005*	.001
Prior innovations	—	.001*	-.001*	.000	-.001*	-.001*
Proportion using	—	-.013*	-.010*	.003	-.008	-.019*
Differentiation and rationalization	—	-1.907*	.492*	-.111	.413	.273*
Involvement of nonmembers	—	-1.177*	.533*	-.109	.453	.082
Privatization of services	—	-.592	.943*	-.333	.146	-.006
Material rewards and incentives	—	-1.313*	.234	2.054*	1.281*	.363*
N	372.000	17,915.000	4,907.000	928.000	939.000	7,806.000
Naglekerke R-squared	.163	.129	.126	.138	.119	.059

* $p < .05$ one-tailed. Size is measured in 100s of members. Age squared is measured in thousands. Reference category for type of innovation is "New rights and entitlements."

the innovation (-.001). Change in membership has significantly positive effects at three stages: "discussing" (2.132), "decided" (3.538), and "in use" (2.334). This means that at each of these three stages in the process of introducing innovations, kibbutzim that are gaining members are more likely to abandon or lose interest in innovations, while kibbutzim that have been losing members are less likely to. Last, size emerges in table A.4 as a consistently negative influence on transitions away from innovations among kibbutzim that are "not considering" innovations (-.144), are in the process of "implementation" (-.241), or are "currently using" them (-.085).

Among kibbutzim reporting that they were discussing innovations, economic crisis has a negative effect on the probability of movement away from their use (-.004). This means that prosperous kibbutzim are more likely than others to drop innovations from consideration after they have begun to talk about them, whereas kibbutzim in economic difficulty are more likely than others to retain interest in innovations once these have been brought up. This result is consistent with the findings reported in table A.3. Both tables indicate that prosperity makes kibbutzim less interested in innovations, whereas economic hardship does the opposite. Both tables indicate that the effects of economic crisis are felt early in the process of considering innovations and are absent at later stages.

As previously noted, prior innovations have, at three stages, negative effects on the probability of movement away from use of innovations. But they also a significantly positive effect on the probability that a kibbutz that was not previously considering an innovation will reject it in the coming year (.001). This result is consistent with the findings of table A.3: prior innovations increase the number of innovations that a kibbutz considers, but they do not increase the proportion of the innovations under consideration that the kibbutz approves.

Differences among Innovations

We would like to add a few comments about the differences among categories of innovations that are shown in the last four lines of tables A.3 and A.4. Our models estimate the effects of each of the four categories of innovations listed, leaving innovations that create new rights and entitlements as the omitted category against which the other four are contrasted. New rights and entitlements are the innovations in widest use, making them also the innovations most frequently considered, and giving negative coefficients in column two of table A.3 to all other categories of innovations (in comparison to these most frequently considered).

Once innovations begin to be discussed, those that involve privatization of services are most likely to make transitions toward use of the innovation (.538), and those that create new material rewards and incentives are least likely to move toward use (-.577). Once innovations have been decided upon, it is, surprisingly, the innovations that involve material rewards and incentives that are most likely to advance toward use (2.315). This is the single instance in which making more radical changes appears to make decision makers more resolute. In table A.4, however, innovations involving material rewards and incentives are found to be the innovations most likely to be abandoned, at three stages: among kibbutzim that had "decided to adopt" innovations (2.054), among those that were in the process of "implementing" innovations (1.281), and among those that had reported that they were "using" innovations (.363).

In the first two columns of table A.4, it is the innovations in the omitted contrast category "new rights and entitlements" that stand out. At the stage of "discussing" innovations, those involving new rights and entitlements are least likely to be dropped from consideration. Strangely, in transitions beginning with "not considering," it is also those involving new rights and entitlements that are most likely to be rejected. This could in part be an indirect tribute to the popularity of these innovations, because innovations need to receive some degree of attention and acceptance to be frequently rejected.

Transitions among Types of Payment

The following analyses present estimates of the effects of a number of predictors on the probability that a kibbutz would switch from "need-based" to "safety-net" or "mixed" forms of budgeting during the years 1995–2005. The predictors in these models are similar to those included in chapter 3. Means, standard deviations, and mutual correlations for these predictors for these years are shown in tables A.5 and A.6. The average kibbutz was 50 years old at the time of these observations, and had 218 members. Age and size are highly correlated with each other (.60). Kibbutzim belonging to the Artzi federation constitute 33 percent of the total. The average kibbutz

TABLE A.5.

Descriptive Statistics for Covariates of Transformations, 1995–2004

Variable	Mean	Standard deviation
Economic crisis	59.89	18.96
Change in membership	-1.64	8.73
Need-based budget	.78	
Mixed compensation	.06	
Safety-net budget	.15	
Years since change	.83	1.91
Age of kibbutz	50.39	16.29
Age of kibbutz squared (100s)	28.04	15.73
Number of members	218.43	133.70
Artzi federation	.33	
Geographic isolation	75.62	57.43
Prior innovations	508.05	505.93
Percent safety-net or mixed	21.70	24.82

Notes: Economic crisis is measured on a scale from 0 (excellent condition) to 100 (severe crisis); change in members is the difference between the reported membership from the year of observation to the next; "Need-based," "Mixed," and "Safety-net" are dummy variables with the value 1 if a kibbutz is of the given form at the year of observation, and 0 otherwise; "Age of kibbutz" is the number of years since the founding of the kibbutz until the year of observation; "Membership" is the membership of the kibbutz at the year of observation; "Artzi federation" is a dummy variable taking the value 1 if the kibbutz is a member of Artzi, and 0 otherwise; "Geographic isolation" is the distance, in kilometers, from the kibbutz to the nearest urban place. "Prior innovations" is an index created by calculating the percentage of all surveyed innovations that had been adopted by a kibbutz throughout the years prior to the current year of observation. "Percent safety-net or mixed" is the percentage of all kibbutzim that had adopted either the mixed or safety-net form at the year prior to the observation. An earlier version of this table appeared in *Advances in the Economic Analysis of Participatory and Labor-Managed Firms* 11 (Emerald Group Publishing 2010).

is located 76 kilometers from the nearest large city (Tel Aviv or Haifa). Kibbutzim in more peripheral locations are on average younger (-.44) and smaller (-.31) than other kibbutzim. The incidence of economic crisis is negatively correlated with the size of a kibbutz (-.21), indicating that larger kibbutzim are on average in better economic condition than smaller ones.

For the years in which the "safety-net" budgetary system was spreading (1995 through 2005), change in size averages -1.64, meaning that the average kibbutz was losing 1.6 members per year. This variable is negatively correlated with age (-.14) and size (-11), indicating that older and larger kibbutzim were more likely to be losing members.

Of other influences, the proportion of other kibbutz reforms previously adopted by the individual kibbutz, and the proportion of kibbutzim that have previously adopted "safety-net" or "mixed" budgets, are strongly correlated both with each other (.68) and with type of kibbutz.

Modeling Transitions among Types of Payment

Table A.7 estimates the determinants of the transitions from "need-based" to "mixed" and "safety-net" budgets. The basic observational design for this analysis is a complete panel of kibbutzim by year over the period 1989 to 2005. The analysis predicts the log odds that the budgetary system of a kibbutz is "mixed" or "safety-net" relative to "need-based" in the year subsequent to the measurement of the predictor variables. For example, the scores of independent variables in 2004 are used to predict the status of the kibbutz in 2005. The total possible sample size for this analysis is 4097, but only 3343 observations were usable due to missing data on some covariates.

Table A.7 examines the effects of a number of covariates on the likelihood that a kibbutz will transform itself from "need-based" to "mixed," from "need-based" to "safety-net," or from "mixed" to "safety-net" in a year of observation (there were no transitions from "safety-net" to either "mixed" or "need-based," or from "mixed" to "need-based"). In these analyses, the pooled panel (kibbutzim by year) is divided into those that are currently "need-based" and those that are currently "mixed." Multinomial logistic regression is used to simultaneously predict the likelihood of transitions from "need-based" to "mixed" or "safety-net" (relative to remaining "need-based"). Binary logistic regression is used to predict the likelihood of transitions from "mixed" to "safety-net" (relative to remaining "mixed").

TABLE A.6.
Correlations among Covariates of Transformations, 1995–2004

	1	2	3	4	5	6	7	8	9	10	11
1. Economic crisis	1.00										
2. Change in membership	-.08	1.00									
3. Need-based budget	-.11	.05	1.00								
4. Mixed compensation	.05	-.04	-.50	1.00							
5. Safety-net budget	.09	-.03	-.81	-.11	1.00						
6. Age of kibbutz	-.04	-.14	-.13	.06	.11	1.00					
7. Age of kibbutz squared	-.04	-.16	-.12	.05	.11	.97	1.00				
8. Number of members	-.21	-.11	.16	-.07	-.15	.60	.58	1.00			
9. Artzi federation	-.05	.03	.10	-.07	-.07	.05	.02	.09	1.00		
10. Distance from cities	-.03	.03	.08	-.02	-.07	-.44	-.38	-.31	-.11	1.00	
11. Prior innovations	.12	-.08	-.70	.30	.60	.24	.25	-.11	-.19	-.12	1.00
12. Pct. safety-net or mixed	.04	-.03	-.60	.20	.55	.28	.30	-.06	.00	.00	.68

Source: An earlier version of this table appeared in Advances in the Economic Analysis of Participatory and Labor-Managed Firms 11 (Emerald Group Publishing 2010).

These analyses are based on complete panels of kibbutzim and years, so more direct approaches to dealing with the nonindependence due to pooling are possible than was the case with the adoption of innovations analyses discussed in the previous section. We adopted the fixed-effects approach of including vectors of intercepts for individual origin years, and for individual kibbutzim (these intercepts are not reported in the tables in the text, to save space).

This approach raises two considerations regarding the results. First, significance tests and estimated standard errors are, most likely, more correct and reliable for this (and subsequent analyses, discussed below) than for the individual-innovations analysis (which may overstate statistical significance). Second, regression coefficients need to be interpreted as effects controlling for kibbutz-specific and year-specific heterogeneity. That is, the regression coefficients take into account that the likelihood of transitions may be systematically higher for all kibbutzim in a given year—or systematically higher in a given kibbutz across all years—for reasons that we regard as unobserved, but nonrandom.

In table A.7, we present a series of models that analyze the effects of these predictors on the probability that a kibbutz with "need-based" or "mixed" budgeting will transform itself into a kibbutz with, respectively, "mixed" or "safety-net" budgeting between one year and the next. The observations are a panel of 249 kibbutzim observed across the years 1995–2004. The models presented are multinomial logistic regressions, with fixed effects for year and kibbutz. Coefficients are additive effects on the log-odds of a transition during a year, relative to the odds of no change. Estimates by maximum likelihood are obtained from SPSSx version 15.0.

For each of the three observed transitions, two models are estimated. In each pair of models, the first omits the number of innovations that had previously been adopted on each kibbutz—which is our measure of organizational inertia—and the second model includes this number. In the first model in each pair, predictors like age, size, and economic condition are allowed to exert their full effects regardless of how that effect is brought about. A given influence might be making an organization more or less likely to make this particular change, as theories of degeneration would lead us to expect, or it could be making organizations more or less likely to introduce changes of all types, as theories of inertia and resource dependency predict. By adding the number of innovations previously adopted by each organization, the second model in each pair attempts to control for differences among organizations in their relative openness to change or inertia. Under these circumstances, the second model of each pair shows the effects of predictors, not on the likelihood of change in general, but on the unique attractiveness to the organization of this particular transformation.

Estimates of the effects of each potential influence on transitions to the "mixed" and "safety-net" types of budgeting are shown in table A.7. The first two lines in table A.7 report the effects of the age of a kibbutz on the likelihood of transformation. Regarding the effects of age, three theories are potentially relevant. First, Hannan and Freeman's (1984) theory of organizational inertia predicts that organizations become less likely to change, the older they become. Second, the literatures on democratic (Weber 1978) and communal (Pitzer 1989) organizations include many reports that these organizations become less democratic and less communal, the older they become; in the literature on producer cooperatives, this view is seen in the older idea that cooperatives have a tendency to "degenerate" over time (Mill 1909). Batstone (1983) adds a third possibility with his theory that periods of "degeneration" in democratic workplaces are often followed by periods of "regeneration." Degeneration followed by regeneration would produce a curvilinear effect for age on change in democratic workplaces, positive for low values of age, negative at higher values. Including both age and age-squared in these models shows the linear effect of age at low values of age, while age-squared shows the effects of age, at high values of age.

For transitions from "need-based" budgets to the "mixed" type, the results shown in table A.7 are consistent with Batstone's theory. The positive but curvilinear relationship predicted by Batstone's theory is indicated by a significantly positive effect for the linear form of age in Model I, coupled with the significantly negative effect for age-squared in Model II. In other models of transitions from "need-based" budgeting to the "mixed" or differential types, coefficients for age and age-squared are similar, but lack statistical significance.

This curvilinear effect of age on the transformation of kibbutzim is consistent with the predictions of Batstone (1983), and can therefore be taken as support for his theory; but it can also with equal justice be

TABLE A.7.

Effects on the Probabilities of Transitions to Mixed and Safety-Net Budgets

	From need-based to mixed		From need-based to safety-net		From mixed to safety-net	
	I	II	I	II	I	II
Economic crisis	.015*	.010	.027*	.023*	.023*	.023*
Change in membership	-.053*	-.044*	-.002	-.013	-.050	-.050
Age of kibbutz	.072*	.070	.057	.043	-.101	-.101
Age of kibbutz squared	-.062	-.074*	-.062	-.072	.097	.096
Number of members	-.003*	-.002	-.004*	-.003*	.001	.001
Artzi federation	-.607*	-.185	-.588*	-.056	.703	.746
Geographic isolation	-.004	-.002	-.009*	-.007*	.002	.002
Prior innovations		.003*		.003*		.000
Percent safety-net or mixed	.042*	.010	.068*	.037*	.028*	.027*
Intercept	-6.166*	-6.679*	-6.205*	-6.824*	-1.968	-2.048

Notes: * p < .05, one-tail.

Multinomial logistic regression coefficients (estimated with SPSSx 15.0), with fixed effects (not shown) of year and kibbutz. Coefficients are additive effects on the log-odds of a transition during a year relative to the odds of remaining in the origin status.

Model I and model II differ only by the inclusion of the prior innovations variable.

Nagelkerke pseudo R2: model I transitions from need-based = .174; model II transitions from need-based = .263; model I transitions from mixed = .127; model II transitions from mixed = .127.

For definitions of the variables and their metrics, see the text and notes to Table A.5.

An earlier version of this table appeared in *Advances in the Economic Analysis of Participatory and Labor-Managed Firms* 11 (Emerald Group Publishing 2010).

interpreted as providing partial support to each of the two other competing theories, depending on which ranges of age are focused on. At low values of age, organizations of intermediate age are more likely to undergo transformations than younger ones, as theories of democratic and communal organizations predict. At higher values of age, older organizations become less likely to undergo transformations than are those of intermediate age. This means that, at these higher ranges of age, organizational inertia does increase with age, as Hannan and Freeman (1984) anticipate, but the predicted effect of age on organizational inertia occurs only at higher ranges, after the contradictory effects of age predicted by Pitzer (1989) and by Batstone (1983) have played out.

Although the effects of age and age-squared in these models are subject to interpretation, the effects of size unambiguously support theories of organizational inertia, not theories of degeneration. The significantly negative effects of size on transitions from "need-based" budgets to both "mixed" and "safety-net" budgets indicate that, as Hannan and Freeman (1984) predict, kibbutzim become less likely to abandon their traditions, the larger they become.

As seen in table A.3 and in other studies (Rosner and Tannenbaum 1987; Simons and Ingram 1997), kibbutzim affiliated with the Artzi federation are less likely than other kibbutzim to depart from traditional practices; this is seen whether we look at transitions from the "need-based" budgets to the "mixed" type or to "safety-net" budgeting. But when the number of innovations previously adopted by the kibbutz is included, estimates of the effect of differences between federations are greatly reduced and lose statistical significance. This result suggests that Artzi kibbutzim are less likely to make these transitions, because they are less likely than Takam kibbutzim to embrace any or all of the recently proposed kibbutz reforms. When this generally greater fidelity to kibbutz traditions among Artzi kibbutzim is incorporated into our models (Model II), Artzi kibbutzim are revealed to show no greater resistance to budget-mode reform than they do to all the others.

Table A.7 indicates that, as theories of communal organizations in general (Kanter 1968) and of the kibbutzim in particular (Ben-Ner 1987) predict, distance from cities makes kibbutzim with "need-based" budgets less likely to transform themselves into "safety-net" kibbutzim. In this case, the effect remains significant, even when the negative relationship between rural locations and the adoption of other innovations has been controlled for.

According to Oliver's (1992) theory of deinstitutionalization, organizations are most likely to abandon institutionalized practices when scarcities of resources make it increasingly difficult to afford their costs. On the basis of this theory, we would expect to find that kibbutzim that are in greatest economic difficulty would be most likely to introduce new forms of compensation. In the literature on communal and democratic workplaces, on the other hand, these organizations have often been accused of becoming more likely to abandon their cooperative structures, the more capital they accumulate or the more profitable they become. Compensation change thus constitutes another instance in which theories of organizations as institutions, and theories of democratic and communal organizations, make contradictory predictions. The results shown in table A.7 are entirely consistent with Oliver's (1992) resource-based theory of deinstitutionalization. The weaker the economic condition of a kibbutz, the more likely the kibbutz becomes to make each of these three transitions.

Demographic crisis also stimulates transitions of kibbutzim with "need-based" budgets to the "mixed" model, but has no effect on the other transformations. This may be due to unique features of the "mixed" type; this form of compensation is essentially a compromise between traditionalists and reformers, retaining "need-based" budgets as the traditionalists want, but also adding market-based differential payments as the reformers want. Which kibbutzim are most likely to choose this compromise? Table A.7 suggests that the kibbutzim that are losing members, and cannot afford to lose any more, are most likely to choose this form of compensation, since it tries to please everyone.

Prior innovations, which serve here as a negative indicator of organizational inertia, behave as expected. The more reforms a kibbutz has adopted in the past, the more likely it is to transform itself from a kibbutz with "need-based" budgeting into a kibbutz of the "safety-net" or "mixed" type. Once a traditional kibbutz has transformed itself into a kibbutz with "mixed" compensation, however, prior innovations have no further effects on whether or not the kibbutz takes the next step of adopting the "safety-net" budget.

Turning to the effects of the adoption of "safety-net" or "mixed" forms of budgeting by other kibbutzim, the first model in each pair indicates that, as expected, such external adoptions stimulate all three transitions. When the number of innovations previously adopted by a kibbutz is controlled for, however, the estimated effect of the adoption of the "safety-net" or "mixed" forms of compensation by other kibbutzim is greatly reduced and, in one case (transitions to the "mixed" type) loses statistical significance. Given that most of the transitions incorporated into this measure are to the "safety-net" budget, not to the "mixed" type, it is unsurprising that the total proportion of kibbutzim that have adopted new forms of budgeting stimulates transformations to the former type of budget more strongly than it promotes transitions to the latter type.

REFERENCES

Abramitzky, Ran. 2008. "The Limits of Equality: Insights from the Israeli Kibbutz." *Quarterly Journal of Economics* 123: 1111–1159.

Admadjian, Christina L., and Patricia Robinson. 2001. "Safety in Numbers: Downsizing and the Deinstitutionalization of Permanent Employment in Japan." *Administrative Science Quarterly* 46: 622–654.

Amir, Yehuda. 1969. "The Effectiveness of the Kibbutz-Born Soldier in the Israel Defense Forces." *Human Relations* 22: 333–344.

Arbel, Shulamit, ed. 2004. *Annual Report of the Kibbutz Movement, No. 3.* Tel Aviv: Department of Economics, the Kibbutz Movement [Hebrew].

———. 2005. *Annual Report of the Kibbutz Movement, No. 4.* Tel Aviv: Department of Economics, the Kibbutz Movement [Hebrew].

———. 2006. *Annual Report of the Kibbutz Movement, No. 5.* Tel Aviv: Department of Economics, the Kibbutz Movement [Hebrew].

Barkai, Haim. 1977. *Growth Patterns of the Kibbutz Economy.* Amsterdam: North-Holland Publishing.

Batstone, Eric. 1983. "Organizations and Orientation: A Life Cycle Model of French Co-operatives." *Economic and Industrial Democracy* 4: 139–161.

Beck, Nikolaus, Josef Brüderl, and Michael Woywode. 2008. "Momentum or Deceleration? Theoretical and Methodological Reflections on the Analysis of Organizational Change." *Academy of Management Journal* 51: 413–435.

Ben-Ner, Avner. 1984. "On the Stability of the Cooperative Type of Organization." *Journal of Comparative Economics* 8: 247–260.

———. 1987. "Preferences in a Communal Economic System." *Economica* 54: 207–221.

———. 1988. "Comparative Empirical Observations on Worker-Owned and Capitalist Firms." *International Journal of Industrial Organization* 6: 7–31.

Ben-Rafael, Eliezer. 1988. *Status, Power, and Conflict in the Kibbutz.* Aldershot, UK: Avebury, Gower Publishing.

———. 1997. *Crisis and Transformation: The Kibbutz at Century's End.* Albany: State University of New York Press.

———. 2011. "Kibbutz: Survival at Risk." *Israel Studies* 16(2): 81–108.

———, and Menachem Topel. 2011. "Redefining the Kibbutz." In *One Hundred Years of Kibbutz Life: A Century of Crises and Reinvention*, ed. Michal Palgi and Shulamit Reinharz, 249-258. New Brunswick, NJ: Transaction Books.

——, with Yechezkel Dar, Yuval Dror, Sigal Ben-Rafael Galanti, Ran Kochan, and Ofri Degani. 2009. *The Kibbutz on Paths Apart*. [Hebrew]. Jerusalem: Bialik Institute.

Berger, Peter, and Thomas Luckmann. 1967. *The Social Construction of Reality*. New York: Anchor Books.

Bettelheim, Bruno. 1969. *The Children of the Dream: Communal Childrearing and American Education*. New York: Macmillan.

Blasi, Joseph. 1978. *The Communal Future: The Kibbutz and the Utopian Dilemma*. Norwood, PA: Norwood Editions.

——. 1986. *The Communal Experience of the Kibbutz*. New Brunswick, NJ: Transaction Books.

Blumberg, Paul. 1968. *Industrial Democracy: The Sociology of Participation*. New York: Schocken Books.

Buber, Martin. 1958. *Paths in Utopia*. Trans. R.F.C. Mull. Boston: Beacon Press.

Charney, Igal, and Michal Palgi. 2001. "Reinventing the Kibbutz: the 'Community Expansion' Project." In *One Hundred Years of Kibbutz Life*, 259–270.

Clark, Shawn M., Dennis A. Gioia, David J. Ketchen Jr., and James B. Thomas. 2010. "Transitional Identity as a Facilitator of Organizational Identity Change during a Merger." *Administrative Science Quarterly* 55: 397–438.

Cohen, Erik. 1983. "The Structural Transformation of the Kibbutz." In *The Sociology of the Kibbutz*, ed. Ernest Krause, 75–114. New Brunswick, NJ: Transaction Books.

Department of Economics, the Kibbutz Movement. 2012. *Annual Report of the Kibbutz Movement, No. 9: 2010 Data*. [Hebrew]. Tel Aviv: Department of Economics, the Kibbutz Movement. Available online at http://www.kibbutz.org.il/calcala/info/shnaton/120403_shnaton9.htm. Most recently accessed September 4, 2012.

DiMaggio, Paul J., and Walter W. Powell. 1983. "The Iron Cage Revisited: Institutional Isomorphism and Collective Rationality in Organizational Fields." *American Sociological Review* 48: 147–160.

Dror, Yuval. 2011. "The New Communal Groups in Israel: Urban Kibbutzim and Groups of Youth Movement Graduates." In *One Hundred Years of Kibbutz Life*, 315–324.

Estrin, Saul, and Derek C. Jones. 1992. "The Viability of Employee-Owned Firms: Evidence from France." *Industrial and Labor Relations Review* 45: 323–338.

Etzioni, Amitai. 1958. "The Functional Differentiation of Elites in the Kibbutz." *American Journal of Sociology* 64: 476–487.

——. 1980. *The Organizational Structure of the Kibbutz*. New York: Arno Press.

Fishman, Aryei. 1992. *Judaism and Modernization on the Religious Kibbutz*. Cambridge: Cambridge University Press.

Friedland, Roger, and Robert R. Alford. 1991. "Bringing Society Back In: Symbols, Practices, and Institutional Contradictions." In *The New Institutionalism in Organizational Analysis*, ed. Walter W. Powell and Paul J. DiMaggio, 232–263. Chicago: University of Chicago Press.

Gavron, Daniel. 2000. *The Kibbutz: Awakening from Utopia*. Lanham, MD: Rowman & Littlefield.

Getz, Shlomo. 1994. "Implementation of Changes in the Kibbutz." *Journal of Rural Cooperation* 22: 79–92.

———. 1998a. "Winds of Change." In *Crisis in the Israeli Kibbutz*, ed. U. Leviatan, J. Quarter, and H. Oliver, 13–25. Westport, CT: Praeger.

———. 1998b. "Changes in the Social and Functional Borders of the Kibbutz." [Hebrew]. *Horizons in Geography* 48–49: 97–110.

Greenberg, Zeev. 2011. "Kibbutz Neighborhoods and New Communities: The Development of a Sense of Belonging among the Residents of New Community Neighborhoods on Kibbutzim." In *One Hundred Years of Kibbutz Life*, 271–287.

Greenwood, Royston, and C. R. Hinings. 1993. "Understanding Strategic Change: The Contribution of Archetypes." *Academy of Management Journal* 36: 1052–1081.

Greve, Henrich R. 1999. "The Effect of Change on Performance: Inertia and Regression toward the Mean." *Administrative Science Quarterly* 44: 590–614.

Hannan, Michael, and John Freeman.1984. "Structural Inertia and Organizational Change." *American Sociological Review* 49: 149–164.

Hardy, Cynthia, and Steve Maguire. 2008. "Institutional Entrepreneurship." In *The Sage Handbook of Organizational Institutionalism*, ed. Royston Greenwood, Christine Oliver, Roy Suddaby, and Kerstin Sahlin, 198–217. Los Angeles: Sage.

Harel, Yehuda. 1988. "The New Kibbutz: An Outline." *Kibbutz Currents*, no. 2 (August): 2–5.

Haveman, Heather A., and Hayagreeva Rao. 1997. "Structuring a Theory of Moral Sentiments: Institutional and Organizational Coevolution in the Early Thrift Industry." *American Journal of Sociology* 102: 1606–1651.

———. 2006. "Hybrid Forms and the Evolution of Thrifts." *American Behavioral Scientist* 49: 974–986.

Helman, Amir. 1980. "Income-Consumption Relationship within the Kibbutz System." In *Integrated Cooperatives in the Industrial Society: The Example of the Kibbutz*, ed. Klaus Bartolke, Theodor Bergmann, and Ludwig Liegle, 131–141. Assen, Netherlands: Van Gorcum.

———. 1994. "Privatization and the Kibbutz Experience." *Journal of Rural Cooperation* 22: 19–32.

Henisz, Witold, Bennet A. Zelner, and Mauro F. Guillen. 2005. "The Worldwide Diffusion of Market-Oriented Infrastructure Reform, 1977–1999." *American Sociological Review* 70: 871–897.

Horrox, James. 2009. *A Living Revolution: Anarchism in the Kibbutz Movement*. Edinburgh: AK Press.

Ingram, Paul, and Tal Simons. 2000. "State Formation, Ideological Competition, and the Ecology of Israeli Worker Cooperatives, 1920–1992." *Administrative Science Quarterly* 45: 25–53.

Jepperson, Ronald L. 1991. "Institutions, Institutional Effects, and Institutionalization." In *The New Institutionalism in Organizational Analysis*, ed. Walter W. Powell and Paul J. DiMaggio, 143–163. Chicago: University of Chicago Press.

Kanter, Rosabeth Moss. 1968. "Commitment and Social Organization: A Study of Commitment Mechanisms in Utopian Communities." *American Sociological Review* 33: 499–517.

Katz, Yossi. 1999. *The Religious Kibbutz Movement in the Land of Israel*. Jerusalem: Hebrew University Magnes Press; Ramat Gan: Bar-Ilan University Press.

Kellerman, Aharon.1993. *Society and Settlement: Jewish Land of Israel in the Twentieth Century*. Albany: State University of New York Press.

Kibbutz Industries Association. 1983. *Annual Report, 1983* [Hebrew].

Kraatz, Matthew S., and E. J. Zajac. 1996. "Exploring the Limits of the New Institutionalism: The Causes and Consequences of Illegitimate Organizational Change." *American Sociological Review* 61: 812–836.

Kressel, Gideon M. 1991. "Managerial Blunders in the Kibbutz Enterprise: The Problem of Accountability." *Journal of Rural Cooperation* 19: 91–107.

Lanir, Josef. 1993. *The Demographic Crisis in the Kibbutz*. [Hebrew]. Ramat Efal: Yad Tabenkin.

Leviatan, Uri. 1980. "Hired Labor in the Kibbutz: Ideology, History and Social Psychological Effects." In *Work and Organization in Kibbutz Industry*, ed. Uri Leviatan and Menachem Rosner, 64–75. Norwood, PA: Norwood Editions.

———, Hugh Oliver, and Jack Quarter, eds. 1998. *Crisis in the Israeli Kibbutz*. Westport, CT: Praeger.

Livni, Michael. 2011. "Ecology, Eco-Zionism, and the Kibbutz." In *One Hundred Years of Kibbutz Life*, 303–313.

Manor, Ronen. 2004. "The 'Renewed' Kibbutz." *Journal of Rural Cooperation* 32: 37–50.

Maron, Stanley. N.d. Kibbutz as a Communal Household. Ramat Efal: Yad Tabenkin.

———. 1991. "Social Changes in the Kibbutz, 1983–1989." *Kibbutz Trends*, no. 1: 39–43.

———. 1992. *The Kibbutz Movement, 1992—Statistical Yearbook*. [Hebrew]. Ramat Efal: Yad Tabenkin.

———. 1994. "Recent Developments in the Kibbutz: An Overview." *Journal of Rural Cooperation* 22: 5–17.

———. 1998. "Kibbutz Demography." In *Crisis in the Israeli Kibbutz*, 1–12.

Marquis, Christopher, and Michael Lounsbury. 2007. "Vive la Resistance: Competing Logics and the Consolidation of U.S. Community Banking." *Academy of Management Journal* 50: 799–820.

Meyer, John W., and Brian Rowan. 1977. "Institutionalized Organizations: Formal Structure as Myth and Ceremony." *American Journal of Sociology* 83: 340–363.

Michels, Robert. 1962. *Political Parties: A Sociological Study of the Oligarchical Tendencies of Modern Democracy*. Trans. Eden and Cedar Paul. New York: The Free Press.

Mill, J. S. 1909. *Principles of Political Economy*. Ed. W. J. Ashley. London: Longmans, Green, and Co.

Mittelberg, David. 1988. *Strangers in Paradise: The Israeli Kibbutz Experience*. New Brunswick, NJ: Transaction Books.

Mort, Jo-Ann, and Gary Brenner. 2003. *Our Hearts Invented a Place: Can Kibbutzim Survive in Today's Israel?* Ithaca, NY: Cornell University Press.

Near, Henry. 1992. *The Kibbutz Movement: A History*. Vol. 1, *Origins and Growth, 1909–1939*. Oxford: Oxford University Press.

———. 1997. *The Kibbutz Movement: A History*. Vol. 2, *Crisis and Achievement, 1939–1995*. London: Valentine Mitchell.

Oliver, Christine. 1992. "The Antecedents of Deinstitutionalization." *Organization Studies* 13: 563–588.

Oppenheimer, Franz. 1896. *Die Siedlungsgenossenschaft, ein Versuch einer positiven Ueberwindung des Kommunismus durch Loesung des Genossenschaftsproblems und der Agrarfrage*. Leipzig: Duncker and Humbolt.

Palgi, Michal. 1994. "Attitudes toward Suggested Changes in the Kibbutz as Predicted by Perceived Economic and Ideological Crises." *Journal of Rural Cooperation* 22: 113–130.

———. 2002. "Organizational Change and Ideology: The Case of the Kibbutz." *International Review of Sociology 12: 389-402*

———, and Elliette Orchan. 2007. *Survey of Public Opinion in Kibbutzim in 2007.* [Hebrew]. Mt. Carmel: Institute for Kibbutz Research, University of Haifa.

———. 2009. *Survey of Public Opinion in Kibbutzim in 2009.* [Hebrew]. Mt. Carmel: Institute for Kibbutz Research, University of Haifa.

———. 2011. *Survey of Public Opinion in Kibbutzim in 2011.* [Hebrew]. Mt. Carmel: Institute for Kibbutz Research, University of Haifa.

Palgi, Michal, and Shulamit Reinharz, eds. 2011. *One Hundred Years of Kibbutz Life: A Century of Crises and Reinvention*. New Brunswick, NJ: Transaction Books.

Pavin, Avraham. 2007. *The Kibbutz Movement Facts and Figures, 2007.* [Hebrew]. Ramat Efal: Yad Tabenkin.

———. 2008. *The Kibbutz Movement Facts and Figures, 2008.* [Hebrew]. Ramat Efal: Yad Tabenkin.

Pfeffer, Jeffrey, and Gerald Salancik. 1978. *The External Control of Organizations*. New York: Harper & Row.

Pitzer, Donald E. 1989. "Developmental Communalism: An Alternative Approach to Communal Studies." In *Utopian Thought and Communal Experience*, ed. Dennis Hardy and Lorna Davison, 68-76. London: Middlesex Polytechnic.

Preuss, Walter. 1960. *Cooperation in Israel and the World*. Trans. Shlomo Barer. Jerusalem: Rubin Mass.

Rabe, Hesketh, and Anders Skrondal. 2008. *Multilevel and Longitudinal Modeling Using Stata*. 2nd ed. College Station, TX: Stata Press.

Rayman, Paula. 1981. *The Kibbutz Community and Nation Building*. Princeton, NJ: Princeton University Press.

Rosenblatt, Z., and Zachary Sheaffer. 2001. "Brain Drain in Declining Organizations: Toward a Research Agenda." *Journal of Organizational Behavior* 21: 1–16.

Rosenfeld, Eva. 1957. "Institutional Change in the Kibbutz." *Social Problems* 5: 110–136.

Rosner, Menachem. 1988. "There Is Nothing New in the New Kibbutz." *Kibbutz Studies*, no. 26 (May): 11–16.

———, Itzhak Ben David, Alexander Avnat, Neni Cohen, and Uri Leviatan. 1990. *The Second Generation: Continuity and Change in the Kibbutz*. New York: Greenwood Press.

Rosner, Menachem, and Joseph R. Blasi. 1985. "Theories of Participatory Democracy and the Kibbutz." In *Comparative Social Dynamics: Essays in Honor of S. N. Eisenstadt*, ed. Erik Cohen, Moshe Lissak, and Uri Almagor, 295–314. Boulder, CO: Westview Press.

Rosner, Menachem, and Nissim Cohen. 1983. "Is Direct Democracy Feasible in Modern Society? The Lesson of the Kibbutz Experience." In *The Sociology of the Kibbutz*, ed. Elliott Krausz, 209–235. New Brunswick, NJ: Transaction Books.

Rosner, Menachem, and Shlomo Getz. 1994. "Towards a Theory of Changes in the Kibbutz." *Journal of Rural Cooperation* 22: 41–61.

Rosner, Menachem, and Arnold S. Tannenbaum. 1987. "Organizational Efficiency and Egalitarian Democracy in an Intentional Communal Society: The Kibbutz." *British Journal of Sociology* 38: 521–545.

Ruppin, Arthur. 1926. *The Agricultural Colonisation of the Zionist Organization in Palestine*. Trans. R. J. Feiwel. London: Martin Hopkinson and Co..

Russell, Raymond. 1995. *Utopia in Zion: The Israeli Experience with Worker Cooperatives*. Albany: State University of New York Press.

———. 1996. "Individual vs. Collective Forms of Sharing Ownership in Israel." *Journal of Rural Cooperation* 24: 67–86.

———, and Robert Hanneman. 1995. "The Use of Hired Labor in Israeli Worker Cooperatives, 1933–1989." In Derek C. Jones and Jan Svejnar, eds., *Advances in the Economic Analysis of Participatory and Labor-Managed Firms*, Vol. 5, 23–51. Greenwich, CT: JAI Press.

———, and Shlomo Getz. 2006. "Demographic and Environmental Influences on the Diffusion of Changes among Israeli Kibbutzim." In Vicki Smith, ed., *Research in the Sociology of Work*, vol. 16, *Worker Participation: Current Research and Future Trends*, 263–291. Amsterdam: Elsevier.

———. 2010. "Antecedents and Consequences of the Adoption of Market-Based Compensation by Israeli Kibbutzim." In Tor Eriksson, ed. *Advances in the Economic Analysis of Participatory and Labor-Managed Firms*, vol. 11: 233–254. Bingley, UK: Emerald Books.

———. 2011. "The Transformation of the Kibbutzim." *Israel Studies* 16 (2): 109–126.

Schneiberg, Marc, Marissa King, and Thomas Smith. 2008. "Social Movements and Organizational Form: Cooperative Alternatives to Corporations in the American Insurance, Dairy, and Grain Industries." *American Sociological Review* 73: 635–667.

Scott, W. Richard. 2008. *Institutions and Organizations: Ideas and Interests*. 3rd ed. Thousand Oaks, CA: Sage.

Selznick, Phillip. 1949. *TVA and the Grass Roots*. Berkeley and Los Angeles: University of California Press.

———. 1957. *Leadership in Administration*. New York: Harper & Row.

Seo, Myeong-Gu, and W. E. Douglas Creed. 2002. "Institutional Contradictions, Praxis, and Institutional Change: A Dialectical Perspective." *Academy of Management Review* 27: 222–247.

Shafir, Gershon. 1989. *Land, Labor and the Origins of the Israeli-Palestinian Conflict, 1882–1914*. Cambridge: Cambridge University Press.

Shapira, Reuven. 1990. "Leadership, Rotation, and the Kibbutz Crisis." *Journal of Rural Cooperation* 18: 55–66.

Shapiro, Yonathan. 1976. *The Formative Years of the Israeli Labour Party: The Organization of Power, 1919–1930*. London: Sage.

Sheaffer, Zachary, and Amir Helman. 1994. *Brain Drain: The Israeli Kibbutz Experience*. Haifa: Kibbutz Research Centre, University of Haifa.

Sheaffer, Zachary, Benson Honig, and Abraham Carmeli. 2010. "Ideology, Crisis Intensity, Organizational Demography, and Industrial Type as Determinants of Organizational Change in Kibbutzim." *Journal of Applied Behavioral Science* 46: 388–414.

Simons, Tal, and Paul Ingram. 1997. "Organization and Ideology: Kibbutzim and Hired Labor, 1951–1965." *Administrative Science Quarterly* 42: 784–813.

———. 2003. "Enemies of the State: The Interdependence of Institutional Forms and the Ecology of the Kibbutz, 1910–1997." *Administrative Science Quarterly* 48: 592–621.

Spiro, Melford E. 1956. *Kibbutz: Venture in Utopia*. Cambridge, MA: Harvard University Press.

———. 2004. "Utopia and Its Discontents: The Kibbutz and Its Historical Vicissitudes." *American Anthropologist* 106: 556–568.

Stinchcombe, Arthur L. 1965. "Social Structure and Organizations." In *Handbook of Organizations*, ed. James G. March, 142–193. Chicago: Rand McNally.

Talmon, Yonina. 1972. *Family and Community in the Kibbutz*. Cambridge, MA: Harvard University Press.

Thornton, Patricia H. 2002. "The Rise of the Corporation in a Craft Industry: Conflict and Conformity in Institutional Logics." *Academy of Management Journal* 45: 81–101.

Topel, Menachem. 2005. *The New Managers: The Kibbutz Changes Its Way*. [Hebrew]. Ramat Efal: Yad Tabenkin.

Vanek, Jaroslav. 1977. "Some Fundamental Considerations on Financing and the Form of Ownership under Labor Management." In *The Labor-Managed Economy: Essays by Jaroslav Vanek*, 171–185. Ithaca, NY: Cornell University Press.

Warhurst, Christopher. 1999. *Between Market, State, and Kibbutz: The Management and Transformation of Socialist Industry*. London: Routledge.

Webb, Sidney, and Beatrice Webb. 1920. *A Constitution for the Socialist Commonwealth of Great Britain*. London: Longmans.

Weber, Max. 1978. *Economy and Society*. Ed. Gunther Roth and Claus Wittich. Berkeley and Los Angeles: University of California Press.

Winer, Gershon. 1971. *The Founding Fathers of Israel*. New York: Bloch Publishing.

Yassour, Avraham, ed. 1977. *Kibbutz Members Analyze the Kibbutz*. Cambridge, MA: Institute for Cooperative Community.

Yoffe, Daniel. 2005. *Concepts in Analyzing Financial Reports of a Kibbutz*. [Hebrew]. Tel Aviv: Department of Economics, the Kibbutz Movement.

———, ed. 2004. *Annual Report of the Kibbutz Movement, No. 2*. [Hebrew]. Tel Aviv: Department of Economics, the Kibbutz Movement.

Zilber, Tammar B. 2002. "Institutionalization as an Interplay between Actions, Meanings, and Actors: The Case of a Rape Crisis Center in Israel." *Academy of Management Journal* 45: 234–254.

INDEX

ABOUT THE AUTHORS

RAYMOND RUSSELL is a professor of sociology at the University of California, Riverside. He has studied participation by employees in the ownership and control of their workplaces in many contexts and countries, including the United States, Israel, and Russia. His previous works on Israel include *Utopia in Zion: The Israeli Experience with Worker Cooperatives*.

ROBERT HANNEMAN is a professor of sociology at the University of California, Riverside. His past research has examined patterns of organizational change in national medical care, educational welfare, and political institutions. He is currently working on the complex dynamics of social network development, primarily for medical and community development applications.

SHLOMO GETZ has been a researcher at the University of Haifa's Institute for Kibbutz Research since 1985, and senior lecturer at Emek Yezreel College since 2006. He is the author or coauthor of numerous books and articles, both in Hebrew and in English, about changes in the kibbutzim.